8/27/01

To Jim Douras —

Very Best Regards

ACKNOWLEDGMENTS

This book is a compilation of knowledge and experience I've accumulated over the past two decades practicing law as a commercial trial litigator and general business counsel, and a full list of acknowledgments would stretch more pages than I could realistically devote. Many people have been helpful along the way, and many names will go unmentioned, so I hope that I'm forgiven.

My special thanks to my wife Susan, for without her this book may not have been written, and to my loving daughters, Alyssa and Alexa, for the time away from them while I gained the knowledge and experience to write this book. The world of asset protection planning is all about them.

Also thanks to my brother Harry "Bud" Etters, Jr. for always being there, and to Jack Allgood for his guidance and direction in writing this book. Thank you to the many, many clients that have given me the opportunity to learn, and to the many opposing litigation attorneys that have allowed me to hone my skills.

Many thanks to all!

ISBN: 0-9706844-0-1

Library of Congress Control Number:
00-093574

Tanzer, David A.
    The complete guide, how to legally protect your
a$$ets: a stateside and offshore planning guide to
wealth preservation techniques / by David A. Tanzer.
    -- 1st ed.
    p. cm.
    Complete guide, how to legally protect your assets
    Includes bibliographical references and index.

    1. Estate Planning -- United States -- popular works.
2. Finance, Personal -- United States. I. Title.
II. Title: How to legally protect your assets III. Title:
Complete guide, how to legally protect your assets

KF750.T36 2001   346.7305'2
                                  QBI00-898

THE COMPLETE GUIDE:
legally
HOW TO ^ PROTECT YOUR ASSETS

A Stateside and Offshore Guide to Wealth Preservation Planning Techniques
By David A. Tanzer,
Attorney at Law

Caveat:

This publication is designed to provide accurate authoritative information in regard to the subject of asset protection planning and wealth preservation techniques. It is sold with the understanding that neither the author nor the publisher is engaged in rendering legal, accounting or other professional service. If legal advice or other expert assistance is required, the services of a competent professional person should be sought.

> *-from a declaration of principles jointly adopted by a committee of the American Bar Association and a committee of publishers.*

Printed in the United States of America. First Edition. First Printing.

Contents

CHAPTER EIGHT
Successful Business Structures

INTRODUCTION-
WHAT YOU WILL LEARN

You can learn to protect your assets. This book is designed for you if you are serious in learning about the many different legal techniques available to protect and preserve your hard-earned money and property. It is about knowing and understanding the many legal tools available to you and how to successfully use these tools every day for your benefit. This book is designed for you if you are interested in both stateside asset protection planning, as well as the best options available for going offshore to protect and preserve assets.

Once you have read and absorbed the powerful information within, you will discover that asset protection planning is more than just transferring assets or setting up Trusts. It is more than choosing between stateside and offshore planning.

You will discover that true asset protection planning integrates both stateside and offshore worlds, is the daily use of state laws and planning techniques, and combines these together with international offshore planning. Real asset protection planning is a "holistic" approach. This means that you should plan the parts consistent with the big picture in mind.

You will learn that asset protection and wealth preservation is designed to level the playing field in a world of plaintiff hungry lawyers and greedy sharks that are out to get a chunk of your assets. Never can you have enough advanced planning to protect and preserve what you have worked hard for, whether your assets are designed for your retirement or for passing on to your family. There is nothing worse than witnessing someone who has worked endlessly for financial security and independence just to lose it all overnight. Especially when that someone is you.

You will receive a wealth of information from this book. Protecting and preserving your assets is your legal right. You need not feel guilty about using these important legal techniques. What you do with your assets, short of defrauding others, is your choice. By doing nothing, you choose to expose your money and property to whoever desires to take it. Instead, by taking action today, well in advance of problems or claims against you or your property, you can protect and preserve your hard-earned money and assets.

So read this book carefully, and you will be among those who have learned to protect and preserve their assets.

For the first time, a complete guide to all of the different legal asset protection tools contained under one cover. Many successful people are using many of these techniques today to protect their assets.

HOW TO USE THIS BOOK

This book is divided into three parts. You will learn how the wealthy use stateside and offshore asset preservation to protect their assets.

Learn from SECTION ONE of this book **THE BASICS OF ASSET PROTECTION PLANNING AND WEALTH PRESERVATION**. This segment is designed to give you an introduction and overview of commonly used stateside tools for everyday living, either in your personal or business relationships. You may be familiar with some of these tools, but you will also be introduced to many new techniques and how to best apply them for wealth preservation.

Discover from SECTION TWO about **PROTECTING AND PRESERVING YOUR ASSETS FROM DISABILITIES & DEATH**. This shorter segment of the book is an attempt to provide the layperson with an overview of how to plan for disabilities and inevitably, death. These tools are customarily found in stateside planning, but when integrated into offshore planning, the results are greatly enhanced. This is an important part of protecting and preserving your assets if you are serious about dealing with some of the inevitable natural disasters that life can bring you and your loved ones.

One of the most exciting parts of this book is the **ADVANCED ASSET PROTECTION PLANNING FOR THE SERIOUS** found in SECTION THREE. The first two segments of the book lay an introduction for the third section, however, it can be read on its own. This third segment takes a closer look at some of the best offshore preservation tools available to you today. Importantly, this part of the book integrates stateside planning tools to gain the best advantages available for asset protection and wealth preservation.

Learn about synergy. The concept of using tools and techniques together is an important part of this book. Think of synergy as the single acorn that grew the mighty oak. An advanced and aggressive level of asset protection planning is not only perfectly legal, but as you will see, being without these techniques leaves you naively vulnerable in a world where wealth accumulation is often lost much quicker than it is created.

For the first time, a complete guide on asset protection planning designed for the layperson. However, professionals acting in the discipline of law, accounting and asset management will find it a useful aid in providing stateside and offshore planning advice to their clients.

Now, you too can give serious thought to protect what you have worked long and hard for. Instead of waiting until you are confronted with a serious problem, act now to protect those assets you have been working so diligently to provide for you and your family. Most importantly, start today.

The key to asset protection planning and wealth preservation, stateside or offshore, is to be proactive if you are truly serious about protecting and preserving your money and property. You must act now!

Best regards,

David A. Tanzer,
Attorney at Law
Vail, Colorado

****

SECTION ONE:

THE BASICS OF ASSET PROTECTION PLANNING AND WEALTH PRESERVATION

(STATESIDE PLANNING)

CHAPTER ONE

Why Asset Protection Planning?

FIRST FINANCIAL BATTLE:
MAKING MONEY

WHAT ARE THE TWO GREAT FINANCIAL BATTLES of life that we are all presented with? It all boils down to just two. Only two.

The first great challenge, in non-technical terms, is to reach the goals and objectives that you have set out to accomplish. That is, reaching your personal goals, making the money. Whether your source of wealth building derives from your own business or working for someone else, or through commissions, or capital gains on the sales of assets, or creating equity in whatever form, the first big financial challenge in life is making money. Plain and simple.

There is nothing wrong with pursuing the first big challenge, as long as it is done honestly and legally. If one of your top priorities is to increase your balance sheet, while you keep your other commitments in life in perspective, this is truly a worthy cause. Building financial security for yourself or your family is something you can take great pride in achieving. This is what the American Dream is all about.

During my years of practicing law and advising clients, I have personally witnessed some basic business plans of clients turn into wonderful financial success stories after years of hard work and dedication. Some of the simplest ideas put into practice have created great fortunes. Brilliance and intelligence often have a limited place in creating these fortunes. Generally hard work and perseverance are the keys to creating great wealth.

How to create wealth and make it grow is the topic of many books. As a young man looking to reach some of my own financial goals, perhaps one of the most influential books to me on this topic was *Think and Grow Rich*, by Napoleon Hill. Setting goals, outlining specific steps to reach those goals, and taking immediate action to accomplish those goals are all critical steps.

There are many good books and basic courses available on how to get rich, if that is your goal. This book goes beyond this first step and seeks to preserve the wealth you are creating.

SECOND FINANCIAL BATTLE: KEEPING THE MONEY

Too often, while focusing on the number one priority of making money, another, perhaps more important financial battle is completely overlooked. When you are so involved with creating and building and making things happen, your focus can completely miss the other great financial battle of life. This is a common error of most successful people.

Again, in non-technical terms, the second great financial battle of life is keeping what you have created. Protecting and preserving your assets is probably the most important of the two battles, and if you are like most people, you probably give little more than passing wind to this challenge.

Litigation Gone Wild

Stop for a moment and think about how litigation in America has almost become a favorite pastime. Plaintiff's legal counsels never seem to run out of creative new theories of liability. And the willingness of judges and juries to embrace those theories is mind boggling, even from extenuating circumstances.

And your Honor, just one more word about nothing new, talking endless hours at someone's expense to get nowhere fast, I say this about that, even though said before in less words, blah, blah...

Remember the recent McDonald's case where a woman spilled a hot cup of coffee in her lap as she sped away from the drive-through window and sued for millions of dollars? The jury awarded her an enormous amount of money for what some claimed was her own stupidity. A spilled cup of coffee or an innocent oversight on a business or professional matter can be worth hundreds of thousands, or millions of dollars, to a creative plaintiff's legal counsel.

Some as-of-yet-unasserted theory of liability, no matter how remote, may become tomorrow's rule of law wiping out your lifetime of hard work.

If you do not believe me, consider this recent case of employee litigation against an employer. A claim was made by a Florida female telephone sex operator that won a $30,000.00 case in which she developed a repetitive motion injury due to masturbating herself up to seven times daily while speaking to clients on the telephone. (Source: National Law Journal April 3, 2000.) Is there much left to your imagination that could not succeed in litigation against you personally?

One of the major roadblocks in our society is the fact that you are a target for litigation. The national average is one lawsuit is filed approximately every 30 seconds against everyday people like you and me. Your chances of getting sued within the next several years are at least 1 in 4. As your asset level increases, so do your chances of getting sued. If you are in the higher asset levels in our country, your risk is even far greater!

RELATIONSHIPS CHANGE

Today's friend can be tomorrow's foe as relationships change. Think back 5 or 10 years ago. How many of your acquaintances then are still close friends today? Even 2 or 3 years ago, how many people have you crossed paths with in even that short period of time?

Has each and every single relationship, however short or meaningful, that has passed through your life ceased to exist in perfect harmony? How many of those people would you continue to trust with personal and confidential information, or even bits and pieces of it that could now be used against you in a lawsuit? Things change and not necessarily to your benefit.

Moving Offshore

In desperation to protect sources of income and wealth accumulation there has been a mass exodus to offshore tax havens to escape from the stultifying national tax system. Greater numbers of normal everyday people are seeking tax havens where hard work is rewarded and not punished by wealth confiscation in the name of taxation.

There is a world of profit opportunities, increased privacy, reduced government interference, and stronger asset protection planning outside of the four corners of the United States, where governmental taxation and interference are not common-place. Americans are seeking these destinations in great numbers.

Loss of Privacy

Individuals continue to surrender their legal rights of privacy and asset protection. Nothing is sacred today, especially with the advent of the Internet. Any information desired by someone looking to get a piece of you is available quickly and easily: health, wealth, tax and marital information, credit history, employment, phone calls, faxes and e-mail, travel, eating and reading habits, even personal preferences when cruising the Internet.

TOO MANY LAWS

Not including state laws, Congress alone has enacted over 3,000 federal criminal prohibitions. There are over 1.8 million people locked away in U.S. jails at a cost per year of over $35,000,000,000 (yes billion, not million). The U.S. has achieved the highest per capita incarceration rate for non-political offenses of any nation in the history of mankind. Over two-thirds of all people in American jails are there for non-violent crimes. In other countries these crimes would lead to nothing more than community service, fines, or drug treatment. No doubt America has become closer to a police state.

Congress has passed increasingly burdensome big brother anti-money laundering laws, banking and reporting requirements in the name of the war against drugs. Your friendly local bank is required to complete a Suspicious Activity Report (SAR) and notify the federal government if they believe there is anything suspicious with your banking practices under the Bank Secrecy Act.

Reporting requirements of transporting monies in or out of the country, even if for a legitimate business or family vacation, in amounts greater than $10,000, results in confiscation and other penalties if not properly reported to the government pursuant to Title 31 USC, sec. 5316.

The burdensome record-keeping requirements of wire transfers of greater than $3,000 is yet another tool which intrudes your personal privacy. You may not realize it, but your friendly banker is charged with the responsibility of reporting your wire transfers in an effort to keep tabs on your activities. Ask him or her, you will be surprised with the response.

The 1988 Know Your Customer rules set forth by the Federal Reserve and complex Bank Secrecy Laws places your bank teller in the position of acting as a policing agent for the Federal Government, intruding daily into your personal affairs. Nothing is private anymore unless you take action to protect and preserve it.

FBI & THE INTERNET

Most astonishing is that it was recently revealed that the Federal Bureau of Investigation is using a superfast system called Carnivore to covertly search e-mail. Carnivore represents a new twist in the federal government's fight to sustain its snooping powers on the Internet.

The FBI can literally scan millions of e-mails per second. Carnivore is connected directly through Internet service providers' computer networks that provide your government with the ability to eavesdrop on all customers' digital communications from e-mail to online banking to Web surfing. Absolutely nothing is sacred in the Internet age.

The Carnivore Internet surveillance system is so super-secret and high-powered that the FBI even refuses to provide detailed information as to its abilities and how it works to the members of the Congress oversight committees. Rep. Bob Barr (R., GA.), a member of the Congressional oversight committee on the Carnivore system, introduced a bill attempting to place restrictions on the FBI's use of the Carnivore and requested more information from the FBI on the new system.

Mr. John Collingwood, Assistant Director of Public Affairs for the FBI, wrote back and refused to provide information requested, but in his response said it was all right to trust the FBI's usage of the high-powered surveillance system (Wall Street Journal 8-10-00 at p. B8). Just trust me? Yeah, right John, the checks in the mail and I am sure you will still love me in the morning!

U.S. Attorney General Janet Reno's response to the Carnivore system was that the FBI should change the name so it did not *appear* so threatening. Are you comforted by how the legal system is reacting to this intrusion into your privacy?

FORFEITURE OF PROPERTY RIGHTS

Governmental forfeitures of your personal property is becoming a horrendous violation of personal freedom and privacy, where it is reported that more than 80% of forfeiture cases of personal property are in situations where individuals are never charged with a crime.

In other words, the laws on the books allow the government to take your property when they suspect wrongful activity, and then later decide if and when they want to charge you with a crime. Mere suspicion has become an automatic license for the police to steal your property. This occurs daily throughout the U.S. to even innocent and honest law abiding citizens.

The collection of laws that interfere with your asset preservation and wealth accumulation could fill this book alone. The fact is that there are many roadblocks and laws that interfere with your asset preservation and privacy in our society. Governmental invasion of property rights by forfeiture laws are stacked against you with the sweeping power of the U.S. Department of Justice and individual state's enactment of property seizures.

The invasion of property rights in America makes the George Orwell prophecy of big brother everywhere at all times seem pale by comparison. The assault on the affluent from lawsuits and taxes is increasing. Government waste, even at a time when talk is of reducing the government debt load, continues at an unprecedented pace, as the many levels of government waste your money daily.

Heavy Taxation

Tax loopholes are closed, followed by more taxation, directly or indirectly. Increased taxes in our society are a grotesque fact of life. The bureaucratic red tape increases even after promises of a kinder and gentler society and less government.

Limitations on Insurance

Even if you have taken care to retain maximum levels of insurance protection, will it cover a catastrophe if and when a problem arises? Will the policy exclude the claim? Will the coverage be sufficient? Will the insurance company be in business and not bankrupt when you need to make a claim?

As the cost of even this limited protection goes up and up and as a result, many business and professional people are over-exposed and grossly under-protected, even with outrageous premiums.

The reality is that there are many roadblocks facing you every single day in your search for the good life. What steps you take, or fail to take, will have great impact upon you and your family for the rest of your life and beyond.

PROTECT YOUR ASSETS

But there are things you can do to preserve and protect your hard-earned assets. Taking action includes some simple, and not so simple stateside measures. Or you can follow the lead of the wealthy and large corporations by going offshore outside the boundaries of the US and take advantage of some of the most liberal jurisdictions that they use every day.

Our lives are in a constant state of flux. Relationships change, governments enact new laws, local and worldwide political climates are constantly taking new avenues, and our financial situations are in a constant state of change. It is essential that you consider what might occur and what events are likely to happen. Then you can analyze the impact that these events might have on your goals and objectives.

It is essential that you plan for alternatives in protecting your money and property, well in advance of a problem. And most importantly, you must implement appropriate techniques to deal with the "unexpected catastrophe" now, and not later.

Let's back up for just one moment and think about the amount of money that passes through your hands. Stop and think about just your personal expenditures alone over the past years, forgetting about all of the many tools you will learn about in this book. You have probably allowed a small fortune to pass through your life already.

Take an easy rounded household income of $100,000.00 per year for two wage earners. Once this was considered an unusually large salary. Yours may be significantly more or less. No matter, the concept is the same. What do you have to show from your source of income over the past years? What unexpected events have changed your plans over the years? How have you reacted? What tools did you have in place to deal with these "unexpected" events? How would you change things?

Before we even discuss the basic tools of assets protection planning, let alone the more advanced levels found later in this book, during an average 40-year income-producing career at an average household income of $100,000.00, you would have earned $4,000,000.00. And this is before you even consider the compound value of money or the opportunities to invest and multiply those funds.

Most people would agree that accumulating $4,000,000.00 in the bank is a handsome prize.

From those monies you have living expenses and taxes and claims of others that certainly affect wealth accumulation during your earning years. But how you go about your affairs, how you manage your life, how you elect to own or hold your assets, will make the difference between how small or how large your balance sheet is when you cross the finish line.

YOUR LEGAL RIGHT

So, what is asset protection planning anyway? Is it a plan or scheme to defraud your creditors? Is it a scam to avoid paying Uncle Sam your share of income taxes? Is it a scheme to deny creditors their due share of your worth? Hardly.

It is important to start from a very important premise before you go any further with this book. The basic assumption is that you too believe that you have a right to do what you want with your assets, as long as you are not cheating anyone else and following the rules. Some may use this book to flaunt the law, and that is always the case. But this book is intended to provide you with insight of useful legal tools to preserve and protect your assets during, and even after, your life.

What does all this mean? Well, you can give your assets away in the form of a gift, either before or after you die. Charity, heirs, beggars and thieves form a long line. Or, you can certainly spend those assets and waste them away on world-wind tours, the fast lane, or conspicuous consumption, if you prefer. Just go for it.

Of course you can always save your hard earned assets for a rainy day in the form of a nest egg, and continue to build your net worth, if this is your goal, and a worthy one at that. There are many things that you can do with your money. It is simply your choice.

WORTH REPEATING

I will say it again: what you do with your assets, your money, your real estate, and your personal property, is your personal choice. What you do with these assets, and how you go about protecting and preserving them, is entirely up to you.

Now let's not get too far ahead of ourselves. If those assets already have a claim against them, or they are collateralized by others for the repayment of a debt, then they are only yours to do as you wish beyond the claims of others. Plain and simple, your assets, subject to the claims of others, do not share the same freedom as those other assets that are free from claims of others.

Chances are that your assets are not 100% collateralized or subject to the rights of others. If your debt is anywhere close to the amount of your assets, then this book is not yet for you. I would recommend that you read a different book, perhaps one on investing, or better yet, on how to manage your cash flow properly.

Understand Your Rights

But I will speculate that since you are reading this book you are well on your way to accumulating and growing your nest egg for your own financial freedom. The freedom and independence to make your own choices in life; to be the captain of your own vessel searching for new ports beyond the horizon.

The only question that now remains is how you can protect those assets from the jaws of hungry plaintiff's lawyers or from the vultures that thrive on greenmail, or the many other avenues that can separate you from your assets.

This book will simplify many different stateside asset protection planning tools and look at some of the best techniques for offshore planning. Importantly, you will see how to integrate the tools together to protect and preserve your assets.

I have had the wonderful privilege over the past two decades of representing a wide variety of clients with respect to their legal and business affairs. I have litigated cases on behalf of plaintiffs trying to strip away assets, naturally only for worthy causes, against villainous defendants. I have righteously defended many a hard-earned fortune from the jaws of do-gooders. I have seen many fortunes made based upon dreams and hard work by some of my best business clients.

And too, I have seen many fortunes squandered away because the client simply failed to take basic protective measures to protect and preserve those assets.

It is from those two decades, also inclusive of teaching at a university in Chicago, that I draw upon to share with you what I have learned from my clients, the smart ones and the not so smart, the successful ones, and the not so successful. But more importantly, it is the past two decades of hard work, perseverance, down in the trenches, hardball legal battles, which create the empirical knowledge from the school of hard knocks. I will share with you some of the legal techniques that I have experienced so that you can protect and preserve your own assets.

I have given numerous asset protection seminars over the years trying to cram asset protection planning techniques into a one and one half-hour program. This is equivalent to not much more than skipping a stone across the surface of the water and hardly touching base on any one issue. The purpose of this book is to go deeper below the surface of the many topics that are considered legal useful asset protection tools. These are tools to use today.

UNDERSTAND THE CONCEPTS

Keep in mind that an entire book could be written about any one of the topics we will discuss, and probably already has. This books condenses those hundreds, or perhaps thousands of books, years of law school education, and the two decades experience of litigation and representing closely held businesses into a summary or overview of the topic called *asset protection planning*.

That means that we will not be able to cover every single legal or business application on every single issue, but that you will at least have a sufficient understanding as to why you should consider any one asset protection tool in your arsenal of weapons as you seek to protect and preserve your assets too.

To draw upon an analogy of sailing, consider yourself on a great sailing adventure through life. What is the first step you

To the starboard, no the port, no wait, hurry up and slow down!

take after you have acquired your choice of sailing vessel? You make plans where you want to sail. Then, you plan for the adventure. Next you equip your sailing yacht with not only the comforts of life, but with a back up plan in case of trouble.

Hopefully you have selected life vests, and a good working communications system, and a life raft "just in case". Unless you are suicidal, you would not set off on a long sailing journey without the basic tools to protect and preserve your life and family.

Asset protection planning is like sailboat racing. All vessels are in the same water, same wind, and same weather. Someone wins, and someone loses. Some weather the storm, and others do not. Often good planning makes all the difference.

PLAN AHEAD

This is what asset protection planning is all about. Planning ahead for the storm. Not if, but when.

When my wife Susan and I did some of our sailing adventures we owned a wonderful 40' Irwin, rightfully named "Master Plan". Sister ships have repeatedly placed in the top ranks in transatlantic yacht racing. No doubt Master Plan was a fine seaworthy vessel. But we still had a life raft that hung over the back, just in case. The name of the life raft was "Plan B", and was always with us "just in case" we needed to step up into the life raft if Master Plan was taking on water.

Obviously the time to go shopping for your life raft is not when your ship is sinking. If you have prepared your Master Plan in life with Plan B essentials, then they are available when you want, or need them most.

Perhaps the most disheartening situations that I can recall while representing clients over the years, are the ones in which the client never bothered to prepare for the certain storms that come along in life. Listening to the unfortunate set of circumstances that fall on the best of people is not always an easy way to spend your day. Too often, by the time most people seek advice on protecting and preserving their assets, there is very little that can be done, other than damage control.

And too, there are those clients who come into the office and talk about asset protection planning as though conversation alone will take care of what they need. Take Mark and Linda (not their real names) who both reached 50 this year; they came into my office again just this past week. He owns a very successful plumbing contracting business, two homes, good nest egg, and has made and spent a lot of money over the past fifteen years. He has been talking about taking asset protection planning steps for the past three years. Never does anything about it, but somehow it must make him feel better just to talk.

The stress of the business is now starting to take a toll on his health in various forms. Even if he only took some small step in the right direction, he would be light years ahead in protecting his wife and three daughters should something serious happen to him. But he just keeps talking about it.

I do not quite understand Mark's reluctance to take action. He has his reasons, but hopefully he won't wait until it's too late.

If only those clients that fail to plan ahead bother to take action while the seas are calm, then they too could have had confidence that their Plan B was ready to step in when they need it most. Remember, now is the time to do something, not when the ship is taking on water.

47

GOALS

Your goals should be to seek out privacy regarding the holdings of your assets, avoid or minimize the impact of lawsuits, eliminate or reduce potential problems with friends, lovers, business partners and associates, avoid unforeseen changes in legal and political climates, avoid imposition of limitations on the free movement of assets, and achieve maximum benefits through tax related strategies.

Great goals, but how do you achieve these objectives?

The legal tools available to you to protect and preserve your assets are many. Some will be just what you need, others will be irrelevant and unnecessary. But most importantly, if the tools are known and you have them at your disposal when you need them, then you can pick and choose, with good legal counsel I might add, how to protect your assets when the time is right.

SECTION PREVIEWS

Remember, this book is divided into three sections and looks at both onshore and offshore opportunities for asset preservation. The first section compiles a long list of tools and concepts that you should use daily in your life. These concepts should affect how you make business decisions, handle your love life, and consider your personal and professional relationships with others. Without belaboring an in-depth analysis, these legal tools, or safety nets, are applicable in your everyday life. You will see how they can benefit you today and in the future, if used correctly.

The second section of this book deals with catastrophes that every one of us will deal with in one form or another. This I can guarantee! Whether we like it or not, we will be confronted with personal and family issues of disabilities, and all of us will eventually be confronted with death. There is no sugar coating, and this is not rated PG. The focus of this section will be on how you can use the many tools available to help minimize the financial hardships and emotional trauma of dealing with these inevitable hardships.

Finally, the third section of this book is for the advanced student of wealth preservation. For those individuals who are in high-risk professions or are well on their way to achieving their financial goals and independence, this is for you. You will explore, first hand, the most advanced and aggressive asset protection tools that are legally available today by going offshore. You will see clear examples of how the extremely wealthy preserve and protect their assets. These tools and techniques are no more foreign than you make them, and are at your disposal now.

SYNERGY

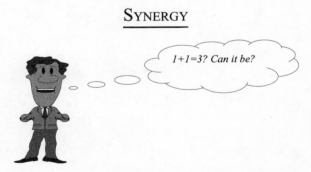

Importantly, as you proceed through this book, think in terms of synergy. One idea plus another idea is not just two.

The synergy, or the combined effect of using tools together, can be best understood as starting with one concept and skillfully integrating it with another concept. The result is a total effect, which is greater than the sum of the individual parts. This individually tailored combination of tools or techniques will allow you to take the fullest advantage of the synergistic relationship. You will see some excellent examples of the combined benefits as we proceed through this book, especially when we arrive at the third section.

Let's now get started and see what tools you have been missing to protect and preserve your assets.

CHAPTER TWO

Taxes and Wealth Preservation

H AVE YOU EVER SEEN SAUSAGE MADE BEFORE?
Even the thought is revolting.

Yuuuck!

What does making sausage and making law have in common? The answer is that neither is a pleasant sight to watch. And, the end results may or may not be palatable to you. Laws are constantly being made, forever evolving, and constantly be-

51

ing challenged and changed. The first step is to keep abreast of the legal tools available to you, particularly tax laws. Keeping what you have earned from the taxman is a first basic step in asset protection planning.

FREEDOM FROM TAXES?

Have you ever stopped to think that our wondrous country was originally formed upon the premise of avoiding oppressive taxation? This is one of the main reasons the settlers from Europe left their homes to reestablish in virgin soil across the Atlantic. Of course you remember the Boston Tea Party and what that stands for!

Before the 1920s there were no Federal taxes in the United States. Not one dollar of Federal tax obligations. Even as recent as 1948, the Federal tax rate was only 2%, and primarily for military purposes. And what has happened since with taxes?

The top 5% wage earners pay 52% of income taxes. Depending on the statistics you follow, approximately 15% of US citizens pay 80% of all taxes. The lopsidedness towards the unequal contribution of taxes continues to grow at an unparalleled level.

TAX BURDENS

Taxes now consume a major part of your assets, directly and indirectly. While federal income taxes consume approximately one third or more of your income (depending on your tax bracket) you can add to federal taxes more state taxes.

And, you often pay sales taxes between 5% and 10% (or more!) when you spend the income that you already paid income taxes on. Doesn't it sound rather strange to you that you are being taxed on money that you spend when you have already been taxed on this same money when you earned it?

Backdoor tax increases hit more and more people every year. These are changes in the tax laws that raise taxes without changing tax rates. Among the foremost examples are limitations on deductions and phaseouts of personal exemptions for taxpayers whose incomes exceed certain levels.

In 1999, more than 4.8 million upper-income taxpayers were affected when they prepared and filed their 1998 tax returns resulting in an 14% increase in taxes, totaling $25.9 billion dollars, in these categories alone. The White House and Congress often approve these measures because raising rates indirectly avoids voters from getting angry.

Then there are property taxes you pay every year, year after year, in the form of both real property taxes and personal property taxes. Taxes on real estate often vary around 1½% to 2% every year (and much more in larger urban areas).

A growing trend in many states is the requirement that you identify the value of your business assets and pay taxes on those items, often to the tune of around 1½% year after year. Again, no matter that you have already paid income taxes on the source of income to acquire those assets, or that you pay more income taxes on the generation of additional income with those assets. You are simply taxed again and again on those same assets, year in and year out!

How about the hidden taxes when you purchase gasoline, or alcohol, or tobacco products? And then there is the infamous social security tax which, with a little political magic in less than a year, went from future bankruptcy to politicians arguing about how to refund the excess from the Federal coffers. What a coincidence that another election coincides with these threats and promises.

Let us not forget about excise taxes, and hidden corporate taxes on the production of goods. And yes, if you sell an asset, real estate or a security for example, there is a capital gains tax that you must pay, which varies in amount from time to time.

THE BIGGEST INSULT

Finally, the biggest insult of all, after you have dutifully paid your taxes every year throughout your life, is that when you die, your estate must fork over yet more taxes based upon the value of your assets. And this can add up to a whopping 55% of the total value of your entire estate that has not already been consumed by the earlier burdensome taxes which you previously paid.

You will see in one of the later chapters, how some people trying to plan ahead by using insurance to pay for these tax burdens, are often making a major mistake by burdening their heirs with hundreds of thousands of additional tax dollars, and how that can be avoided.

In 1997, the last year for which data was made available, estate taxes were imposed on approximately 480,000 estates and the average estate tax bill was roughly $430,000.00. More and more families are paying estate taxes today than ever before due to inflation and a decade or more of a healthy economy. And the richer you are, the more you pay. The top 6% of all estates paid $10,390,000,000.00 in estate taxes, and the remaining 94% paid $9,996,000,000.00 in estate taxes in this one year alone.

While there has been an ongoing discussion of repealing the transfer tax, I doubt you can bank on this on-again, off-again tax issue for long, since it is a major source of revenue. Some experts are even speculating that the exemption amount could be even lower after the elections.

Congressman Gephart has long argued his opposition against the middle and upper class and even wants the exemption reduced to only $200,000.00. Apparently, Gephart, and others like him, do not believe that your hard-earned money belongs to your family after you die.

I don't know about you, but where I come from all of this adds up pretty close to 100% taxation! When is the next tea party in Boston?

Hello Slave

Property and wealth determine power to control our own lives, to make decisions, and to live free. Every additional tax diminishes our freedom.

Successful people in the US labor under an annual combined, federal, state, and local tax burden of more than 50% annually. During the Middle Ages, the medieval serfs bound to the land and controlled by their masters rarely paid more than one-third of the value of their labor in taxes. It was for very good reason they were not taxed heavier. With nothing to lose, they would revolt and kill the tax collectors.

Today, some 500 years later, you have fewer rights in the US than those enslaved serfs had, since you are not free to own the product of your labor.

I'm mad as hell and I'm not gonna take it any more!

Year after year the Internal Revenue Service seems to get more creative in collecting taxes, notwithstanding the new image of "kinder and gentler". One such ingenious example, in Freck vs. IRS, No 90-2141. M.D. Penn. (12-3-92) the IRS argued that the taxpayer was both a spouse and not a spouse, strangely winning on both arguments.

The taxpayer filed a joint return but alleged innocent spouse relief pursuant to IRS Section 6013(e). The taxpayer lived with her "husband" in various states, none of which recognized common-law marriage. Thus, the court stated, she did not qualify as a "spouse" under state laws and could not qualify for innocent spouse relief. Notwithstanding, she was still held liable for unpaid taxes as a spouse, since she earlier completed a joint tax return with her "husband" and taxes remained unpaid.

AVOIDING TAXES

What do taxes have to do with asset protection planning? Hopefully this is pretty clear to you by now. With all of the wonderful opportunities that politicians and bureaucrats have to separate you from your assets, good *advanced* tax planning is essential. And I emphasize advanced tax planning for a very good reason. Too often so-called tax experts are really doing nothing more than counting the beans after the fact. What is absolutely critical is that you are making decisions today that help you legally avoid incurring taxes in the future.

As so eloquently stated by Supreme Court Justice Judge Learned Hand:

"Over and over again courts have said that there is nothing sinister in so arranging one's affairs as to keep taxes as low as possible. Everybody does so, rich or poor; and all do right, for nobody owes any public duty to pay more than the law demands: taxes are enforced, not voluntary contributions. To demand more in the name of morals is mere cant." (Commissioner vs. Newman, 159 F2d. 848 (2d Cir. 1947)).

There is a distinction between tax avoidance and tax evasion. Tax avoidance is your legal right to keep your tax obligations to a minimum. Tax evasion, on the other hand, is an illegal attempt to avoid those legal obligations that you owe. Taking each and every legal maneuver that you possibly can to avoid and minimize taxes is your legal right.

SOLID TAX PLANNING

The bottom line is that good, qualified tax planning to minimize future tax obligations is essential, yet surprisingly rare. One of the most important asset protection tools in your toolbox is hiring a top-notch tax planner who can save you big money in taxes.

Too often people fail to get good advice in advance because they are simply trying to save a few dollars by going to their long-time friend that has been doing the same old tax return year after year. Penny wise and pound-foolish. Getting top qualified tax advice, and following it, oftentimes pays for itself over and over again.

Getting second or even third opinions, which can often vary, is further assurance that you are protecting your hard earned assets from unnecessary tax burdens. Of course if you are one of those rare zealots that desire to personally assist in reducing the national debt on your own, I congratulate you.

For the rest of us, getting top qualified tax planning advice is a very important and essential first step to protecting and preserving our assets.

If you have not thought about how your place of residence affects your taxes, you should. There are some states that are more generous to wealth preservation than others.

For example, Alaska, Florida, Nevada, South Dakota, Texas, Washington, Wyoming, Tennessee and New Hampshire have no income tax on wages, and only tax interest and dividends. Perhaps if you are considering relocating to another state within the U.S. you might consider one of these state "tax-havens" more suitable to your needs. You will also explore in Chapter Nine how different states can drastically affect your assets if you are considering bankruptcy, and how to plan ahead by choosing the right state to live in.

U.S. Supreme Court Justice Louis D. Brandies, provided one

small example of how he legally avoided a small, but irritating tax:

"Where I live in Alexandria, Virginia, near the Supreme Court building, there is a toll bridge across the Potomac River. When in a rush, I pay the toll and get home early. However, I usually drive outside the downtown section of the city, and across the Potomac on a free bridge. If I went over the toll bridge and through the toll without paying I would be guilty of tax evasion. However, if I go the extra mile and drive outside the City of Washington to the free bridge, I am using a legitimate, logical and suitable method of tax avoidance. And, I am providing a useful social service as well."

If you have not done so already, go out now and start asking local tax planners who the top experts in their field are. Interview three or four or more of these experts. Ask specifically how they can assist you in the future in reducing your tax burden by tax avoidance. If a tax planner cannot provide you with definite ideas based upon what you do, or are planning to do, keep looking.

The IRS Audit

And importantly, if you are one of the unfortunate taxpayers to receive the IRS audit letter, it is essential that you seek out someone that is well experienced in handling audits and tax cases before the IRS. This is not the time for Mr. Friendly, but the time you realize that your tax expert must have good "moxy" and know the rules inside and out. He or she must know how to weave through the maze of the IRS jungle and to quickly resolve your tax issues to your benefit.

59

You as a taxpayer have legal rights. Find someone that knows these rights and what to do or say, and what not to do or say. Tax avoidance is your legal right and a first step in protecting and preserving your hard-earned assets.

TO SUMMARIZE

A starting point with asset protection planning is to understand how constantly changing tax laws affect you. Both direct and indirect taxes take a big bite out of your wealth. Then, after you die, estate taxes can erode a lifetime of hard earned money. Working with top tax advisers is essential for wealth preservation.

But proper tax planning is only a starting point in protecting and preserving your assets. Once you make money or acquire property, what can you do to keep them?

CHAPTER THREE

Discouraging Lawsuits

W HAT DOES A BAD PERSONALITY AND A GOOD
lawsuit have in common? Too often, too much. What
does this mean to you?

PRINCIPALS

I have sat dutifully across my desk, year after year, case
after case, listening to self-fulfilling prophesies that my client's
case is supposedly based upon principles, and that the money
is only incidental. The principle is always so important, at least
until my first bill arrives for legal services rendered. What a
reflection upon life it is when the pen in hand placed upon check
on desk is mightier than the sword of the most cavalier litigator. You get the point.

The picture in my mind of Mr. Butlows remains vivid. A large, burly, financially successful, retired fellow who was CEO of several large businesses during past years. Your first impression of this man was that he was a charming and harmless teddy bear. But after the doors closed, he made it clear that when he is angry he wants the world to know that what Butlows wants, Butlows intends to get.

If someone was not ready to acquiesce to his demands, long and costly legal action was certain to follow. Butlows at first paid his bills because he had a principle to adhere to that he believed others must follow, whether they liked it or not. But after he became involved in litigation and the costs started running up, he looked for easy ways out to keep his costs down.

Unlike Butlows, I have had the privilege of representing some of the most decent and respectful people who somehow found themselves in a situation not of their own choosing. These unfortunate, hard working souls would just as soon have their wisdom teeth removed, as they would proceed with their unfortunate dispute. Yes, bad things do happen to good people.

EGOS

But too often, bad tempers, ill manners or hardheaded individuals with oversized egos, are simply looking to get the edge up on their adversary.

You can bet your sweet ass I have principles to stand upon!

This is probably what got them into trouble in the first place. They have lost control of the situation, and now they seek to leverage themselves to a superior advantage over another for their benefit. This is what litigation is about. It simply replaces the old fashioned days of seeking "justice" or revenge over another by stepping off ten paces, turning, and firing a pistol upon the other magnificent ego to determine who is right or wrong. Now that was justice!

Butlows was such an irritating person when angry, who was always trying to "lay down the law" on everyone else, that often times his adversaries took a firm stance against him just out of principle of their own. No matter that the legal or monetary issues were insignificant when you boiled it all down. A principle was a principle, and Butlows and his adversaries had to lay claim to their position.

SEEK WIN-WIN RESOLUTIONS

The key here, for asset protection planning purposes, is that too often disputes can be avoided or resolved between people if a win-win situation is sought. By seeking to resolve matters in a positive fashion, instead of trying to control the other fool, you can potentially save your own assets by staying out of the courtroom. Needless to say, large attorney's fees and costs can be avoided. Why place more of your own assets at risk needlessly?

Although not prescribed as a good litigation tactic, sometimes simply picking up the telephone and genuinely speaking with an open heart to resolve matters once the piss and vinegar is exhausted, you can bring quicker and far better rewards than can the best team of expensive litigators playing hardball litigation. Why roll the dice on winning or losing some or all of your assets just because the ego is large or because you believe that justice must be made on this case this very day?

Setting aside over-exhausted calls for principles or large egos to control someone else, is perhaps one of the most important ways to avoid placing your assets at risk. And as you are well aware, litigation costs big bucks.

When you are on the other side of this loser, do you not take some extra pleasure in going after the "jerk"? So, why make yourself the jerk in the next dispute and become the desirable target to go after? Simply stated, everyone likes to get a piece of the big ego or trim down the idiot to size, for whatever reason. Do not be someone's motivating force. Keep the big picture in mind.

And even when you are right, what about this forever-elusive system called "justice" that you seek?

STRAWS OF JUSTICE

One such incident of justice at its best was discovered by a young, female associate in our office. She was only out of law school for perhaps a year. She had all the makings of an excellent litigator, and was well on her way making a name for herself, even at a young age. She gave everything to her clients, and then some.

The young, female lawyer worked hard on resolving an important litigation matter for our client. The laundry list of necessities was long. On the day of trial, the lawyers picked up again with negotiations and the trial was temporarily set aside since settlement discussions were progressing. Actually, the better part of an entire day was spent carving out the fine details of every single important issue for the respective clients. By late in the day, she had successfully resolved every single issue, but for one.

Like a good attorney, she presented to the presiding judge that settlement had been reached except for one very important issue and that a ruling was needed by the judge on this one final point alone. The judge reached into his drawer on the left and pulled out two straws. He then reached into the drawer on the right and removed a pair of scissors. He deliberately cut one of the two straws shorter than the other in full view of the two clients and their astonished attorneys. Litigant A drew first, and justice was final!

Admittedly the drawing of the straws was a rare treat into this judge's decision making process, as well as an unorthodox approach. On one hand, decisions made by some judges, when they finally get around to making them, too often are result orientated and justified upon principles of law to support the decisions. Or, on the other extreme, some judges are more concerned with technical issues of law rather than common sense resolutions to your real life situations. In either case, this gives rise to the saying that good law makes bad cases.

AVOID THE COURTROOM

Have you ever stopped to think about the control that this one man or woman, the Judge, has over your life in a lawsuit? The day before the judge sat high and mighty upon the bench, he or she was just one more dumb old lawyer trying to make a living practicing law. He had the same old cash flow issues and daily grind as everyone else.

Then one day he adorns himself in that black robe and walks into the theater called the courtroom. He suddenly is bestowed with greatness and wisdom, and his affection is the goal of every other attorney seeking rulings in their favor, and they call him "*Your Honor*". Then worst of all, he or she starts to believe that they have been transformed into a new role of high and mighty. Your Honor, many have earned this title, some have not.

And too often juries react on emotion even though they are told not to do so. Frequently, they simply do not understand the law they are supposed to follow. While most jurors have good intentions and seek to do well, it is simply not a perfect legal system.

The point is, do you really want a judge, or twelve jurors, that know little about your life, making financial decisions that you have to live with forever? Do you really wish to drag into the courtroom your personal friends and business associates to help you prove you are right and this other person is wrong? Perhaps there is a time and place for this, but only as a final resort.

Significantly, you should first seek to resolve differences outside of the courtroom, whenever possible. As simple as this sounds, too often the client needs to prove that he or she is right, or an attorney is trying to establish that he or she is the better litigator than opposing counsel, and the case goes on and on at your cost.

Remain Likable

Now we all know that you should have been the winner of the most recent popularity contest, or at least runner-up. You actually won the "humble-citizen" award just this past year. So, you are not the least bit concerned about a large ego getting into your way, or needs for power or control over your adversaries. So what about you? How can you make yourself a smaller or less desirable target when you think everybody wants a piece of you?

Remain Low Key

Another important way of making yourself less desirable as a litigation target is not to be so visible. The more obvious you are, or visibly you display your wealth, whether through conversation or conspicuous consumption, the more obvious a target you become. Do you really need all that attention?

For those that find themselves in a business or profession

that seems to draw bad people looking for good things, and usually your good things, there are legal ways you can hold and control assets that will minimize your risk and exposure to losing them. Much of the rest of this book is devoted to these examples.

What is important about this chapter is that you understand that you need to make yourself a less desirable target. Not seeking to become the jerk of the year that controls the rest of the jerks is a great start. For others, it simply means playing down the role.

LIFE TO THE FULLEST

There is the story of the young businessman sitting on the park bench in great despair. This old man sits down beside him and asks why he seems so distressed. The young man complains about all of the things that are just not going right in his life. The old man says, "That's great!" With a puzzled look the young man asks the old man to explain.

"You see" says the old man, " when you are alive and living life actively involved in many things, it is certain that a percentage of those activities will go astray. The more actively you are living life, the more challenges that come along. It is natural. And the only way that you can avoid all problems is if you are buried six feet below ground. So, rejoice, you must be living life to its fullest!"

So if you are actively involved with many people and activities, no doubt that you too, will experience a certain percentage of them that will go astray. Over time, you too will be disappointed with a friend or business associate that does not deliver what you expect.

Playing Hardball

No doubt, as a last resort, there is a time and place for hardball litigation measures when you need them. However, the local attorney that handled your last real estate closing, or Uncle Jimmy's divorce, may not be the one to turn to. Instead, seeking out a top quality litigator that is well experienced in your area of dispute is critical. Undoubtedly, all lawyers are not created, nor do they practice equally.

Like the young man in the park, for those moments you are convinced that you must be living life to its fullest, there are many techniques to help you ward off your adversaries. Looking for alternative legal techniques to hold and control those assets becomes critical if you are serious in trying to protect and preserve those assets you have worked long and hard for. As you progress through this book, see how many fresh ideas you come up with that might help you protect and preserve your assets. Remember the concept of synergy.

Of course, like the young man on the park bench, you might be convinced that you might die and have no more problems. Lucky you. But, as you will later see, dying has its own set of problems, in more ways than one.

CHAPTER FOUR

Personal Guarantees
&
Debt

ANOTHER SIMPLE BASIC TOOL IN ASSET PROTEC-
tion planning is to avoid personal guarantees. There
are many ways that you can become personally obligated
in your business pursuits. I will assume that you were smart
enough in the first place to establish a separate business entity
(as discussed in Chapter Eight) to avoid personal liability. And
if so, why did you then agree to personally guarantee the business obligations?

PITFALLS

Let me guess at some of your excuses: Your business space
was a good deal or a great location and the landlord would not sign

the lease without your personal guarantee; or, you needed a new fleet of vehicles or new equipment to operate, and the leasing agent would not finalize the desperately needed deal without your signature guaranteeing the lease; or, your friendly bank is pleased to loan you the money to expand or cover cash flow needs, but needed your signature as a routine part of closing the transaction.

Need we look further as to the reason you might personally guarantee a business obligation?

Why is it that so many business people believe that it is routine to place their personal signature on their business' transaction? If the business fails, or if the loan becomes unpaid, everything you personally own is now on the line to repay that loan. You first established the business as a separate entity, perhaps a corporation, to avoid this personal obligation, but then you destroyed this very purpose by giving your personal guarantee for the corporation's debts.

FICTION

First, let's destroy the concept that personal guarantees are absolutely required. They are not. I have represented many successful landlords and a large commercial banking institution with numerous branches throughout the state. I have personally owned many square feet of office space, industrial space, retail space, and executive homes. No doubt, getting the personal signature in case the business fails is greatly sought after all of the time.

However, what is generally sought, is not always accomplished, at least in the personal guarantee department. During the confidential discussions between attorney and client, I have often listened to personal confessions of how that personal guarantee was desired, but also how willing my client was to do the transaction, with or without it.

In other words, even though the personal guarantee was held out as mandatory, they desired the business even more and were often willing to compromise instead of losing the deal. I have personally compromised on obtaining personal signatures in leasing my own property when a good prospective business tenant came along, particularly if the space had been sitting vacant for a while.

CREATING FLEXIBILITY

Mr. Link sought additional office space for his expanding business operations. While he was negotiating for office space in a highly desirable business location, he learned through the grapevine that two other large important tenants were not renewing their leases and this added empty space could arguably create a glut of space in the building. Mr. Link used this fact as leverage in negotiating his new lease and created a new corporation as the lessee, which would then lease back to his business. The lessee corporation had virtually no assets and its limited purpose was to act as the tenant under the lease and pay certain expenses associated with the office space.

Mr. Link had provided no personal guarantee under the office lease, and the business itself was not on the lease. Years later when Mr. Link sought to again relocate elsewhere as the economy slowed down, he simply folded the corporation, acting as lessee, and walked away from the lease in the middle of the lease term without further liability to the landlord.

The landlord had no recourse in this situation, since neither Mr. Link nor his business acted as guarantors or as lessees under the lease. In this situation, both the business and Mr. Link avoided any liability for the actions the corporate lessee created, for the purpose of acting as the tenant under the lease agreement.

LOOK FOR OPTIONS

Avoiding personal guarantees comes in many other shapes and sizes as well. Sometimes, sweetening the deal with additional collateral will get you off the hook. Other times, you might need to pay a premium in the form of a higher rate or rent. And even if you believe that you are forced to personally sign on that next deal, you can always seek to step down the obligations over time.

For example, you might be personally obligated 100% for the first year of a five year term; then, assuming you are not in default, your obligation decreases to 80% the second year; 60% the third, and so on, until it disappears, even though the lease or loan continues thereafter.

Too often, an individual undertaking a personal obligation does not even bother to negotiate this point. They simply sign. The smart ones seek out alternatives. They look for the edge that they are offering the lender, leasing agent, or landlord, and drive home how this is a good deal for them. Then looking to save the deal, they seek alternative ways to avoid the personal guarantee altogether, or too at least minimize their exposure to the greatest extent. It works more times than you will ever realize! But, if you do not ask, you will not receive.

It has been told that hockey great Wayne Gretzky once said "You miss 100% of every shot you do not take." So, if you do not ask for the deal, you will never get it.

And if you have already given personal guarantees, you should make it a top priority to pay them down as quickly as possible. If you anticipate the need to carry out the term of these existing personal guarantees and are unable to pay them off quickly, look for alternatives to replace the loan or lease with another that eliminates or reduces your exposure. You might be surprised; it is sometimes easier than you think to protect and preserve your personal assets by eliminating personal guarantees.

STAY POSITIVE

What about if you have already given your personal guarantee, and the business or property that you own is starting to flounder? Can you reduce your exposure to what you have already provided to the bank or leasing agent? Is it too late to renegotiate your position and protect your personal assets that will be on the line when you are in default? There are options here too.

First, there is an old adage which says if you owe the bank some money and cannot pay, then you have a problem. But, if you owe the bank a lot of money and you cannot pay, they have a problem. If you owe the bank a lot of money, your goal will be to try and assist them with their problem.

According to Mr. Michael Brown, a good friend of mine who manages one of the Alpine Bank branches in the Vail Valley community, *"When a banking customer is in trouble and admits it, and is willing to seek a positive resolution, it is only human nature to want to work with that customer."* Unfortunately, the opposite can be true when a difficult person is unwilling to be honest and cooperate in finding a win-win situation.

Helping your friendly bank, or leasing agent, or landlord out of their problem takes many forms. But whatever the situation, it requires you to be both upfront and cooperative. Too often, the debtor thinks that the more distant, uncooperative, or conniving he or she is, the better their position. This usually compounds the problem.

How do you help someone out of their problem when you owe them large amounts of money? If the lease was for business space you can try and help lease the space. It might even require you or your employees to freshen up the space by painting or cleaning, and even running an ad, or locate a leasing agent to assign or sublet the space for you. Oh wait, you say that your lease prohibits that activity? No problem.

SUBLEASING

Notwithstanding what the terms and provisions of your business space lease indicates, most states have adopted some version of what is referred to as the Suitable Sub-Tenant Doctrine. That is simply fancy legal language which says that the landlord must allow you to mitigate your damages by finding another tenant as a suitable sub-tenant. The new tenant must be at least as able to service the lease and pay as you are. This is promising, considering if you are about to default!

You cannot dump a loser into the landlord's lap. But if you find him a new suitable sub-tenant and he refuses to accept them in your place, it is a great defense against later claims if the landlord tries to sue you for rents due and owing. In other words, the landlord is creating his own problem by being unreasonable in accepting a suitable sub-tenant which you present to him. He cannot later claim you are the bad guy.

The above scenario is required of a landlord in commercial leasing situations, since the laws demand that they mitigate their damages. This means that they cannot be unreasonable in accepting a substitute lessee if you need to get out of a leasing arrangement. But remember that you, too, must be reasonable in finding a substitute and the sublessee must perform, or you will continue with exposure under the lease, unless the landlord is willing to accept the assignment and let you out of the lease altogether.

Resolving Troubled Loans

And what about loans to banks that are in default? By being upfront and cooperative, and trying to assist the lender with turning the asset over to them for resale, you can often preserve a great deal of the value of the asset and minimize your exposure. Sometimes the asset, whether real estate or equipment, can be resold at or near the loan amount, sometimes even more (but do not count on that happening too often!).

In any event, you can oftentimes negotiate a buy-out of a loan or lease. In other words, even though the asset might fall hundreds of thousands of dollars below the amount of the obligation, you might be able to convey the asset to the bank or lender, along with a payment of hard cash, and be relieved from any further obligation.

I think the solution to our problem is as follows…

TURN LOSSES INTO PROFITS

In one such situation, my client had purchased a commercial building for approximately $2,000,000.00. The debt owed was about $1,500,000.00 and was personally guaranteed. He had bought out his partners over several years with cash flow. The cash flow from the rental income was strong and generated a healthy income after all expenses were paid and debt was serviced. In the early years, all profits were poured back into the building as new improvements.

Things changed. First, the real estate taxes on the property over about a five-year period almost tripled. They went from approximately $36,000.00 per year to a smashing $96,000.00. Even though the taxes were being challenged with the local county assessor's office, they first had to be paid, then challenged, and later if my client succeeded, wait several years for a refund. This was the first unanticipated challenge in managing this commercial property.

Then, the rental market collapsed. Not only had there been a building construction surge the previous several years, bringing many new empty buildings in the area onto the market, but the general economy was sagging. It was difficult enough to lease any space within 20% of the prior rental rates, but trying to pass along the increased real estate taxes to prospective tenants was almost impossible.

Due to increased expenses and real estate taxes, decreased rental income, the poor economy, and other factors, the property could not even be sold for half of what it was purchased for five years earlier. The loans far exceeded the value. Improvements and repairs on the property suffered, and eventually my client went into default on the loans.

Fears of taking a personal loss in excess of $1,000,000.00 for this young, budding entrepreneur were incredibly stressful. He had a young, beautiful wife and two small children, having recently moved up into a large home in an upscale community. Fears of everything tumbling down all at once were real. Having to lose the investment was difficult enough, but thoughts of personal bankruptcy loomed heavy.

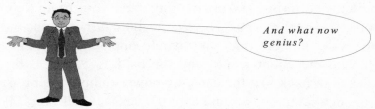

And what now genius?

The first thing we did for this client was to meet with the two banks. He had also convinced another bank to take out a second mortgage to the tune of about $75,000.00, to help with the "short term" cash flow problems when things starting getting rough. Of course, this was also personally guaranteed. It was explained to the bank, who was in the second position, that if he filed for bankruptcy, which was a serious consideration, they would get nothing, particularly since the two loans on the commercial property greatly exceeded the present fair market value.

After considerable hardball negotiation, the second mortgage lender agreed to greatly reduce the debt obligation owed to them, for nickels on the dollar, and the client would raise the money by refinancing a new loan with this same bank on a small condominium he owned in the area. Something was better than nothing.

We then insisted upon this arrangement being contingent upon working out a deal with the first lender. Why? If we could not work out a successful buy-out plan with lender number one, then why bother with lender number two? And, we wanted to make a friend to keep on our client's side. Remember the rule in Chapter Three is to discourage lawsuits?

Now the hard part began. After months of default, repairs on the building suffering, and positioning in the courtroom for over a year, a final deal was cut. The client would turn over the building to lender number one, they would operate and eventually sell it, and the client would pay the bank $45,000.00 for its troubles. The bank had the carrying power to hold the property until the market turned around over the next several years. They would get their money back, and perhaps then some. The client was fully released from the large first mortgage lender, and both banks went on their merry way.

Actually, this transaction worked out very profitably for the client. Since the real estate was an S-Corporation, the pass-through losses worked to offset the client's taxes on other income and investments in future years with some very aggressive tax planning. So, he made money during the good years on the property, negotiated a successful resolution on the two defaulted loans, and then all of the losses, paper and real, were used to offset personal tax obligations in future years. It was a win-win situation after all!

I can hardly recommend that you actively look for the aforementioned way to get out of personal guarantees or to cut your taxes. It took a very tough spirit to ride out the storm and get positive results. It does not always end up that way. The best practice is to avoid personal guarantees in the first place. But, if you've taken on these personal guarantees, either pay them off as quickly as possible, or try to restructure them as soon as possible with new lenders, leasing agents, or landlords.

Use Debt Wisely

Benjamin Franklin set forth two very important rules for life: *"The second Vice is Lying, the first is running in Debt."* Like personal guarantees, debt can be very troubling when business slows down. Mr. Franklin would probably be stunned by American's love affair with debt nearly 250 years later.

In a nation that once saved all it could and resisted taking on debt, Americans today load up on borrowed money to purchase stock, groceries, vacations, pay monthly electric bills, and even borrow money to pay their federal income taxes! Americans have gone on an unprecedented borrowing binge in recent years, even as the U.S. Government is starting to slash its own debt obligations.

The amount of debt that Americans have taken on is startling. According to the Wall Street Journal, a record $4.5 trillion in debt has been accumulated by U.S. non-financial corporations, up 67% in the last half of the 90's decade. Household borrowing has risen 60% percent to $6.5 trillion.

Adding to debt for purposes of good solid business expansion can be a wise decision. But borrowing for consumption, and taking on personal guarantees, is an ugly position to be in as the economy slows down.

Avoiding personal guarantees, like eliminating non-essential investment debt, is another early and basic step in protecting and preserving your assets. Avoid them!

Now, where do you think love and the law meet? Read on!

CHAPTER FIVE

Personal Relationships
& Your Wealth

HOW PERSONAL RELATIONSHIPS CAN DESTROY YOUR
WEALTH ACCUMULATION

AHH YES, LOVE IS A MANY SPLENDORED THING. And how easy it is for fools to fall in love. No doubt the perfect lover helps make the journey through life a fun-filled adventure. The emotional bond and connection, the personal growth, and accomplishments: they are boundless. For those who are fortunate enough to have found such a perfect mate that will stay forever, you can skim through this chapter. For everyone else, read on.

What happens when love goes astray? What about the relationships that end and the lovebirds go their separate ways?

DISPOSABLE SOCIETY

The reality is that 50% or more of all marriages end in divorce. One-half. And the 60's generation that brought acceptability to living together without the benefit of formal ceremonial marriages, suffer even a higher drop out rate. So okay, you

think it will not be your relationship, but some other couple. Ever notice that the emotions on the flip side of love are very bitter, hateful and vengeful? Neither love nor its antithesis is thought-out, rationalized, or logical-thinking, but the legal ramifications are plenty.

What are the issues of love and the law? At what point does ladylove and the law meet?

LIVING TOGETHER

First, when a non-married couple move into a home and live together, start paying rent, or contribute towards a mortgage on a home, jointly take on household expenditures and creditors, or perhaps place separate income for household expenses or savings in common accounts, they are establishing an important legal relationship together. This is true whether they realize it or not.

Importantly, when one of the two parties own the home they live in and the other contributes "rent" paid towards the other's mortgage, this non-legal title holder may, over time, take a legal interest in the home. This possibility becomes even stronger if this non-owner makes improvements or decorates the home and adds any value to it.

The law provides various special legal remedies to protect that person's contributions and added value to the home. The legal doctrines of Constructive Trust, Unjust Enrichment, and Quantum Merit are just a few of the routes that disgruntled ex-lovers have taken to successfully obtain financial benefits to property that they never owned and perhaps were never intended to own.

When the two of you sign up with both of your names to operate the home with the gas company, for electric services, water and sewer charges, or perhaps credit card obligations for "conveniences", or other credit accounts, what happens when you break up and the other person does not pay? Simple: you are legally obligated for the bills. Why? The answer lies in the fact that when you first placed your name on the application form with your live-in, you both agreed and guaranteed to pay the charges.

Your creditor does not care who pays, you are both obligated to pay the outstanding balances. And if you don't, then your credit standing will suffer.

Unless one of the two parties is going to live without any contribution towards the "rent", not make any decorations or improvements to the other's property, not become financially obligated on common household expenditures or credit accounts, then the odds are reduced substantially. I say substantially, but not necessarily eliminated, since successful arguments under similar situations have been made for years about "services" which were provided that had value to the other, and that this non-paying lover should be financially compensated for these services. Right!

DOCTRINE OF UNJUST ENRICHMENT

Recently, in a court case that was sealed from public view by the court, well known racecar driver Danny Sullivan was sued by his ex-lover and live-in girlfriend in Aspen, Colorado. Even though the trial court held that they were not legally married by ceremonial or common law, it granted relief to his ex-girlfriend on the basis of the added value she contributed to his home in Aspen and an expensive Porsche sports car based upon the legal doctrine of "unjust enrichment" (Nini v. Sullivan, 23 FLR 1127 (Colo.Dist.Ct. Pitkin Cty. 1996)).

The Sullivan case demonstrates that courts are willing to seek alternative remedies for live-in partners even when ceremonial or common law marriage is not found to exist.

COHABITATION AGREEMENTS

A simple document that each and every non-married couple should have before they first place their heads on the pillow in the new bed, is called a Cohabitation Agreement. You should spell out how much each contributes financially, and what it is to be used for.

Importantly, you should spell out very clearly that in fact the money paid to live in the same home is "rent" and not a contribution towards the mortgage of the other. And improvements and decorating, even if the home increases in value, does not give rise to a claim in the home or property of the other.

Indemnification against the other against any household credit accounts, or common charge accounts, is essential. That way you can proceed in court against your ex for their share of unpaid amounts due and owing, assuming that you can locate and extract money from the deadbeat.

Better yet, avoid joint credit accounts altogether and reflect any inequities in the amount of the "rent" payment. That way you can make certain that you pay what is in your name and not worry about your lover's failure to meet their obligation.

The Cohabitation Agreement should spell out each and every financial obligation that arises between the two of you. And significantly, it should set forth what happens on the financial side of the relationship in the event it fails, however unlikely you believe this to be.

One of the great benefits of thinking through how to unwind a relationship from the start, is that both parties will know exactly where they stand from the beginning if it becomes unglued. When love is in the air, what better time to sit down and communicate and openly talk about these things. If you can not do it then, when else?

Do you think that when the bitterness and spite set in at the time of a break up, you can really deal with these important matters? Don't worry, you will still have other things to argue about, but at least your finances are in order!

Now if the above arguments are not enough to motivate you to take action to protect and preserve your assets from a disgruntled ex-lover, lets try another approach.

COMMON LAW MARRIAGE

How about the 27-year relationship of Cathy and Stan.

Cathy and Stan first met on a ski trip in their early twenties, fell in love, traveled and eventually moved in together without the benefit of a ceremonial marriage. Their first home was sparse and basic. Money was tight. Stan worked extra jobs to pay the rent. Cathy handmade curtains to hang on the windows to make it a home, and she also worked odd jobs. They had food to eat. They struggled financially, but this was young love at its best.

Time went on, and Cathy and Stan moved into a second rental home together. Income was better, furnishings improved, travel and entertainment were now in the budget. In fact, a common household checking account was established (and was in place for the entire relationship), and each contributed to it on pay-day.

Then a third, fourth, and even a fifth home were shared between the couple as the years went on. They worked hard. Both Cathy and Stan had started their own businesses; had several over the years, and income was now more consistent. They were making long term plans to buy property together and build their dream home. They saved their money together, even established credit to buy the dream property for the perfect home. They were certain that their relationship was special and was going to last forever.

Cathy and Stan bought their dream property together in the mountains with money borrowed from her parents. They bought the land in joint tenancy, which provided that in event of death of one of them, the other would take all. In the early years of making their dreams come true, they lived comfortably in the garage to save money to build their castle, along with some hard work of their own.

Cathy and Stan made important common decisions together, known as "partnering", in conducting their life and personal affairs. Many of their friends simply assumed that they were married, not knowing otherwise; although this was disputed by some of his friends at trial. Mail was received in the name of Mr. and Mrs. by some sources, and their favorite waiter at the best restaurant in town even called them by Mr. & Mrs.

The dream home was all it was meant to be. Grandeur and magnificence. Stan by now was very successful in his business. Of course there were some hard times between them, but like a true couple in love, they endured and survived the worst of times.

Eventually Stan's business was providing him with income of up to $500,000.00 per year. He now had investments outside of the businesses that too were proving successful and providing handsome returns. He was now worth several million dollars, even by conservative accounting, and lived life to the fullest.

Cathy had a small boutique in town, and while not providing much income or having much value, she was happy with the independence. All of Stan's businesses and investments were in his name. Cathy's boutique was in hers. By all accounts, Cathy and Stan had achieved the great American dream during their 27 years together.

Then, as these things sometime go, something happened. The love and affection for one another was no longer strong enough to hold the two of them together during the tough times. He moved out and left her in the big home, along with major expenses to keep it functioning. Since Stan had secretly built a new home elsewhere, he wanted Cathy out of their joint home so that he could get the equity out and reduce his overall expenses.

Stan and Cathy just turned 51 this past year. Stan was convinced that he and Cathy had something special, but that they were merely lovers, boyfriend and girlfriend, over their 27 year relationship. They could have gotten married, he says, but they elected not to; this was their choice.

Cathy, on the other hand, believed that there was something

more, much more, and that they conducted their life as any ceremonially married couple would. Stan filed a suit in District Court to force the sale of the home and evict Cathy. Cathy filed her response in Common Law Marriage, since the state they lived in recognized such legal relationships as marriage.

THE WAR

Both parties were convinced that they were right and the other was very wrong. Cathy and Stan spent over two and one-half years in a bitter legal fight that made the "War of the Roses" look like a trip to the amusement park. The emotion and legal positioning was non-stop. The legal fees and expenses went far beyond their worst nightmare.

The trial lasted almost two weeks, dragged out over a four month period, and approximately 25 friends and neighbors were called to testify as to what they believed the relationship to be. Three expensive experts were called to set forth their opinion about value of assets and concerning the relationship.

The Judge heard the testimony and the parties waited and waited over a one and one-half year period for his ruling as to whether or not there was a common law marriage. Would Stan be forced to share with Cathy half of his hard-earned fortune? Or would Cathy, whose now bankrupt little boutique and only source of income, walk away with nothing? Time seemed to come to a standstill and drag on forever!

If you were the judge, how would you rule?

While the parties continue to wait, you can only ask what

could have been done so that Stan and Cathy each could have protected and preserved those assets realized over the 27 year relationship. Could Stan have isolated those assets from Cathy in the event they went their own ways? And could Cathy have taken protective measures to protect herself from a winding down of this relationship? The answer to both questions is most definitely yes.

COHABITATION AGREEMENTS IN ACTION

Stan could have, and should have had in place, eons ago, a Cohabitation Agreement. Not only would this have resolved financial issues regarding the home, but it would also have protected his business assets and other investments that were created during his 27-year relationship with Cathy. He was the breadwinner in this relationship. He worked, sometimes with and without support from Cathy.

And importantly, since Cathy had agreed to collateralize the home, of which she owned one-half, for a large business loan for Stan, the importance of spelling out and amending the Cohabitation Agreement became even more essential as time went on.

And Cathy could easily have taken measures to protect her interests as well. Since she was relying on his representations that they were as "married as married could be", and Stan's financial success was important for both of their future retirement together, that walk down the aisle in earlier years would have been helpful, no doubt. But since the state they lived in clearly recognized the union of a man and a woman by common law marriage, she had a legal right to rely upon this law.

If she would have sought competent legal advice in earlier years concerning how this legal doctrine arises, she could have made certain that each and every legal step was met and documented, "just in case". Cruel ways to bond a relationship you say? Hey folks, this is real life stuff!

Justice is Slow

As of this writing Stan's and Cathy's lives are still on hold waiting for the court to rule. The wheels of justice are slow and frustrating. Stan's fortune is tied up, and the level of Cathy's future financial security and retirement is uncertain. You want to know the answer, and so do they.

But does getting married solve all of the answers to financial questions? Certainly not.

Prenuptial Agreements

What about when one of the parties bring significantly more assets into a marital relationship than the other? Or, what about if you or your soon to be spouse have children from a prior marriage? Who gets the assets in the event of a divorce or death? If the surviving spouse gets remarried, will this new lover get everything, or even half, in the event they later divorce or your spouse dies?

Can the kids from the prior marriage be protected? How about if the two of you later divorce, do you need to lose half of your assets to your new soon-to-be ex spouse?

Prenuptial Agreements are often frowned upon because, it is

93

claimed, they cast a dark cloud over the love and affection that is being enjoyed between the parties. And, starting out a love affair that is intended to last forever, with thoughts of divorce someday, is negative and focuses the couple with a poor outlook from the beginning. Hum bug I say!

The union of a couple in ceremonial matrimony brings with it significant financial responsibilities. This is particularly true where there are unequal assets brought into the picture or children from an earlier relationship. Is this new, legally binding relationship a gold mining function for one of the partners? Or is it really true love? If it is true love, then let's put the cards on the table.

What was the attraction in the marriage in the first place? If not money, then let's make that clear on a written document. If the other party truly does not want your assets, then get their signature on the Prenuptial Agreement already. Let's keep things honest from the get-go.

A Prenuptial Agreement is a very important and useful tool in protecting and preserving your assets. However, they are not foolproof. The law places a very tight set of standards on the formation of these asset protection tools, and if they are not properly satisfied, then they become a useless piece of paper.

But even that said, they still provide a strong psychological incentive to settle a dispute, since the time and cost to open them up in court during a divorce can be overwhelming, particularly to a weaker party, or someone in a hurry to a new relationship.

The laws vary somewhat from state to state on the formation of Prenuptial Agreements. But the common ground in most states requires full disclosure of all assets, valuable consideration paid to the party with fewer assets, and not be entered into under duress.

The Forever Bride

I remember so well poor little rich girl Cindy Lee. She called me in tears on the evening before her third marriage to a very wealthy businessman. He was now insisting, for the first time, that she sign his Prenuptial Agreement on the day before they married. "How could he?" she asked.

No matter that before her two prior marriages, our office had prepared similar agreements to protect her wealth from the preying claws of her two soon to be ex-husbands. Only difference is that hubby number three was now worth much more than she was.

Perhaps two years later I received the inevitable telephone call from Cindy Lee. Yes, divorce was in the making and could the Prenuptial Agreement she signed the night before the ceremony be broken? Our office argued that not only was the agreement prepared by his lawyer not well-drafted, failed to make a full and complete disclosure of all of his assets, failed to provide valuable consideration to her (that's fancy legalese to say she was not paid to enter into the agreement), but she was under duress to sign the papers the night before the wedding.

A very good settlement agreement was reached for poor Cindy Lee on the doorsteps of the courthouse. No doubt, she was in love, but also a good businesswoman in choosing her partners.

EXPERT ADVISE

Does this mean that Prenuptial Agreements are worthless? Hardly the case. It is absolutely essential that before you say the inevitable "I do", you first sit down with a well qualified, experienced domestic relations lawyer. And importantly, most law-

yers fresh out of law school find that they can quickly build their new law practice by doing divorce work. This is simply because once a lawyer practices for a few years at such a head bashing type of practice, they leave and move on to something a bit more congenial than guerrilla warfare.

So the key essential is to search out the very few domestic relations lawyers that have elected to stay in this field as a specialty (bless their souls) and are seasoned with experience, not a young lawyer just a few years out of school.

THE CANDIDATES

Are you a candidate for a Prenuptial Agreement? According to a **Business Week** article written March 3, 1997, you are a candidate if you own a business, have children from a previous marriage, have a lot of assets, are supporting your spouse through professional school, or have serious success prospects. If you fall into any one of these categories, you should run to your favorite domestic relations lawyer (the well-experienced one) before you walk down the aisle.

And one small bit of reassurance for the faint hearted on this issue. If your beautiful or handsome dream machine fails to walk down the aisle with you after you nicely gift-wrap and present your Prenuptial Agreement well in advance, it was probably for the better. Look at this agreement as a reconnaissance mission to flush out the enemy and see their true colors.

If you are unable to work through an important and essential asset protection tool now, when everyone is lovey-dovey, then when else?

Let's not forget the importance of providing for children, if they are in the picture. If your money matters to you, then how about making provisions in the Prenuptial Agreement for children of a prior marriage? This tool is a very useful and important vehicle for estate planning as well. You should consider using this along with a well-executed set of estate planning documents so that the kids are protected in the event of divorce or death.

All is Fair

Whoever first said that "all is fair in love and war" was on the right track. Relationships change, things happen. If you die before you divorce, that's good news, since your love lasted during the marriage, or at least did not end up in divorce court. But think of Prenuptial Agreements, just like Cohabitation Agreements, as an insurance policy. They are there if you need them, just in case. Then let true love blossom and grow, and the other less wealthy partner will share in the financial rewards anyway.

If the business side of personal relationships does not get your attention to protect and preserve your assets, then how about structuring your business pursuits in the world of blood thirsty sharks? Read on.

CHAPTER SIX

Owning Property With Others

A NOT TOO DISTANT COUSIN OF EITHER LIVE-IN or marital relationships, is co-ownership of property based upon a more traditional business relationship. Most people know that if they desire to have a property pass to them upon the death of the co-owner, then joint tenancy is the way to go. This is true for live-in relationships, husband and wife, or in business situations.

JOINT TENANCY

But, is joint tenancy really and always the best? You will see in this chapter and in the later chapters on estate planning, that this may well not be the best way of holding title in many situations.

Joint tenancy, with rights of survivorship, is simply a legal tool to hold title between two or more people, and provides that if one dies, the others take all. Each have equal enjoyment and use to the property. For two single people or for business partners, this could spell disaster. If you died tomorrow, would you really want your assets to go to your friend, or lover, or business associate? What about your family or other heirs?

Placing ownership in tenants in common might be a better solution, since the property would pass according to your estate plan, or intestate to your heirs if you have no Will. (And if you have no Will, you best speed along with your reading and get to the chapters on Estate Planning!)

Even if you are married, how good of a device is joint tenancy for you? Many states have passed laws, some recent and others long ago, that provide a far better vehicle for co-ownership between married couples. Many couples place their marital home in joint tenancy thinking that they are providing for the other in the event of their death.

While the above is true, it has limitations. For estate tax reasons, this may be a huge and costly tax mistake. (This is later covered in detail, in the chapter on minimizing your estate taxes). And for asset protection planning reasons, there is a better tool to use for many married couples.

TENANCY BY THE ENTIRETIES

Tenancy by the Entireties is a special tool available to married couples for co-ownership of their home. For those couples that do not have a need for additional estate tax planning, this is a superior way to hold title between husband and wife on the marital home. If one dies the other takes title just like joint tenancy.

But, not only can one spouse not sell the home without the permission of the other during their lifetime, generally the claims against only one spouse cannot be attached against the marital home. This may provide a very significant benefit to the couple.

HOMESTEAD EXEMPTIONS

What is important, is that in all states you have a homestead exemption, in the event you file for bankruptcy. Depending on the state you reside in, your homestead exemption varies greatly (see Chapter Nine: Surviving the Financial Crisis). However, in many states, the amount of the homestead exemption protection against creditors is relatively nominal.

The dollar amount of the exemption ranges from several thousand dollars, to perhaps ten or twenty thousand dollars, and in a few states, much more. But owning property in Tenancy by the Entirety could greatly raise the amount of your homestead exemption protection in your state, providing superior preservation of your assets.

For example, let's say that the husband has several business ventures and one fails. The creditors then sue the husband. One of the assets they are trying to reach is the marital home. The husband is forced into bankruptcy. However, since creditors cannot attack the ownership rights against one spouse in a marital property held in Tenancy by the Entirety in many states, the wife and the marital home are protected from the husband's creditors.

In essence, the above resulted in raising the amount of the homestead exemption by the value of the equity in the marital home. This example assumes that the wife was not a co-debtor and that homestead exemptions in the marital home were not waived.

You will need to check with your legal counsel for what your particular state law says about using Tenancy by the Entirety, but this tool is available in many states as a tremendous step forward in the asset protection planning arsenal. I have often stated that if a real estate attorney fails to recommend Tenancy by the Entirety to a married couple in a real estate closing transaction in a state where this valuable tool is available, he is committing malpractice.

Too often, I have witnessed the failure of good legal counsel to provide this tool for their clients because they simply do

not understand it. If this is available to you in your state, consider changing your ownership now, so long that it does not interfere with other federal estate tax planning techniques.

Business Relationships

Non-married couples hold title together in real estate in many situations other than lovers living together. In some circumstances it is a business relationship for whatever reason. Long term plans to hold or develop property, for example, may change as circumstances for one or the other changes over time. What do you do if you need to get out and want to sell the property but the other does not?

Almost all states provide for a legal doctrine known as the Rights of Partition for the Sale of Property. This simply means that absent an agreement to the contrary, one co-owner in real estate can force the sale of the property upon the other and against his or her wishes. This allows one co-owner to get out of a real estate owned property and prevents the other from holding that other co-owner hostage. Rights of Partition for the Sale of Property is an absolute right in most states.

Joint Tenancy Agreements

But what if you do not desire that a co-owner force the sale of real estate upon you? Or perhaps you take title with another person or transfer a portion of the title to a co-owner and you wish to place restrictions on the rights of use, or upkeep or sale of the property. If so, you can enter into a Joint Tenancy Agreement that takes many shapes and forms. They all boil down to setting forth rights and restrictions to the use and sale of the property. They can also set forth formulas to determine value or payment, if one wishes to sell or buy the other out.

Joint Tenancy Agreements should identify the property, and

importantly, the term that you would intend to own if you want the duration of ownership fixed. It should identify under what circumstances you can accelerate a sale if this is desired, and how and by whom, this decision is made.

At what standard will the property be maintained and how will that be paid for? If one party desires to buy out the interest of the other, how will the valuation occur? Will you obtain one or more appraisal? Will the price be determined based upon cost of another measuring device? And will the sale be cash, or in payments over time? What about in the event of death? How will first rights to buy occur if your co-owner dies? Will there be restrictions on use by either party and rent derived from this use?

These and a seemingly endless list of other provisions should be addressed with competent legal counsel.

SENIORS & SYNERGY

Joint Tenancy Agreements go beyond the traditional use of business partners. Remember, think synergy. Thinking synergy is one of the goals of the book. For example, how can a Joint Tenancy Agreement be used in a situation where an elderly person might provide for their future personal care needs and living arrangements with their adult children or grandchildren? What follows is one example of how *not* to make it work.

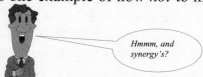

Hmmm, and synergy's?

Grandmother was getting up in age and desired to spend her

final years in her long established home. She and grandpa, when he was alive, put everything they had into their home. Spending the final years of her life in this house had a powerful emotional meaning to her and her well-being. Mom, the oldest daughter, agreed to move in with Grandma after her husband recently passed away.

To free up some cash, Grandma sold one-half of the home to Mom at a discount price and gifted one-half of the remaining one-half interest to grandson retaining the other fourth interest for herself.

Grandma understood that the lesser sales price for one-half interest in the home was in exchange for Mom's care of Grandma in the home during her final years of living. Grandma also provided by Will that Grandson inherit the remaining one-fourth interest after her death. Grandson, recently became an adult, and now lived in the same home with Grandma and Mom. Three generations all under one roof living in peace and harmony?

When Grandma reached her final twilight years, the health care needs and attention were an increasing burden for both Mom and Grandson. Both had employment outside of the home and Grandma's medical needs required constant daily attention that they could not provide. Mom set out to sell the home to raise cash to place Grandma into a nearby nursing home.

Grandma was livid, and not willing to participate in the sale. Grandson took the side of Grandma. As co-owner in the home, Mom filed a case in court based upon her legal right to force the sale of the property under a Partition suit.

THE TRIAL

Standing side-by-side before the judge in open court were three generations. Mom, as plaintiff, sat on one side of the courtroom. Grandson pushed Grandma into the courtroom in her wheelchair and sat on the other side before the judge. The drama that unfolded for this family and their many friends was played out through their testimony during a week long trial.

In the end, the court agreed with Mom that there is an absolute right to force the sale of property as a co-owner. The only issue left for the judge was to figure out a scheme for the distribution of money once the sale of the home was completed. Not a very good form of asset protection planning on anyone's part, since legal fees and expenses on both sides, combined with the appointment of a receiver and real estate broker, ate away at a considerable amount of the equity upon the sale of the home.

PUT IT IN WRITING

Grandma could have, and should have, entered into a Joint Tenancy Agreement, which provided for the terms of conveyance, and placed use and restrictions upon the home. Importantly, a non-partition provision should have been inserted into the agreement prohibiting or restricting the sale of the home.

With the aging of America, and many families having the greatest part of their estate tied up in their homes, providing for the care of the elderly continues to become more and more of an issue. The equity of a home is a great tool for providing for elderly care, but preserve it wisely.

Before we shift gears, let's look at one more method of caring for the elderly and providing for their needs, while protecting and preserving assets for the next generation.

CHAPTER SEVEN

Assets of The Elderly

LATER IN THIS BOOK WE COVER A NUMBER OF different types of Trusts, their purposes and benefits. But since we looked at caring for Grandma in the last chapter, we will take one more look at an asset protection tool for the elderly and address it briefly. It is called a Medicaid Type Trust.

Medical care for the elderly, and for the not so old, is and will certainly remain a hot topic for the years ahead. The baby boomers are quickly aging and their health care needs will only continue to grow. It is expensive to stay in a hospital, and doctor visits and medication are almost off the affordability charts for the seriously ill or elderly.

Staying insured with health care for a young family, is equal to taking on another mortgage, and becomes almost impossible as you grow older.

MEDICARE

Medicare is a governmental program that provides medical insurance for people over 65. Like social security, it has become an institution and has its share of bureaucracy and problems. It actually provides two insurance programs: one is automatic for anyone that qualifies, Part "A" coverage, and another is optional coverage for a fee, or Part "B".

MEDICAID

Medicaid, on the other hand, is designed to provide medical care for older, low-income Americans. This is also a federally-sponsored program that takes over when these elderly have no income or assets left to provide for their own care. Medicaid pays for about 50% of all nursing home costs nationwide, but is extremely expensive and extremely controversial.

Elderly who anticipate lengthy nursing home care in the future have sometimes tried to speed up their qualification for Medicaid. The motive is generally to preserve some of their assets for their children instead of spending all of their money on the nursing home.

MEDICAID QUALIFYING TRUSTS

In the past, they have tried to give their assets to family members, set up an irrevocable trust to hold the money for their use, or for the inheritance of the children. In recent years, those transfers made within 36 months before applying for Medicaid would not allow qualification. So, the transfers are generally made prior to the required 36-month period to qualify, and ultimately protect and preserve assets.

Medicaid Qualifying Trusts have come under major attack in recent years. On one side, the opponents claimed that they are a sham, a fraud, and should be disallowed. The proponents on the other side argued that a party has a right to do as they wish with their assets, and that using a system that they contributed into for many years was their legal right. Both sides have presented persuasive arguments along these lines.

The Law

To curtail the formation of Medicaid Qualifying Trusts, Congress has passed recent laws making deliberate and intentional spending down of an estate, for purposes of qualifying for Medicaid, a federal crime. It is now illegal for a financial or legal advisor to help you devise such a plan, even though you, or your elderly parent, wouldn't be charged with the crime.

Congress struggled with the concept, or at least the bad publicity, of hauling off to jail the frail elderly, for the law that took effect in 1997, and decided to go after the estate planners instead.

Options to Qualify

An elderly person can still qualify early on for Medicaid if the law is not violated. Remember that a major philosophy of this book is that as long as you are not defrauding, hindering or causing delay of payment with current or anticipated creditors, you have a right to do as you wish with your hard earned assets.

Spend your assets freely if you desire; give them all to charity if you prefer; better yet, help pay down the national debt and do without good tax planning. Or, if you prefer, give them away to family, well in advance of anticipating a need to qualify for Medicaid. Your family can place these assets in a Trust, outside of your use or control, and supplement your needs in later years if they so elect.

However, keep in mind that once you gift these assets away to your family, the assets are out of your control and use, and are no longer yours. They are left in the control of others as to how they will be used and spent, and sometimes this presents a set of problems in itself. And too, the issue of gifting must be dealt with wisely for federal tax purposes.

While I do not wish to leave you with an impression that I am indecisive with using Medicaid Qualifying Trusts, I do wish to reiterate that great caution and advance planning must occur when you use these types of planning techniques, when attempting to directly qualify for Medicaid. Planning years ahead before Medicaid is needed to indirectly achieve the same results is the key to asset preservation for children and family members of the elderly.

PLAN AHEAD TO QUALIFY

Unfortunately, due to the changes in the law, you will be unable to obtain good expert legal advice on directly qualifying for

Medicaid. But, you can accomplish the same results by another name and gifting your assets in early years to third parties. Then place the assets in a luxury type Trust for your benefit and obtain full discretion as to how those assets are later distributed. No doubt there are risks associated with this planning, since the assets are no longer in your name or in your control.

Nonetheless, if you can deal with the above issues in a proper and legal fashion, you too have an opportunity to protect and preserve your assets, or that of your elderly family member, for future generations. Then, you have an opportunity to benefit from a federal medical program that was created with that person's hard earned tax dollars over many years of contributing into the system.

Gifting from one generation to another is just one more piece of the puzzle and has many benefits if used wisely and planned for early on. The key is to plan ahead and not wait until the assets are actually needed. As with most other asset protection and wealth preservation techniques, it must be planned for well in advance. Think of it as purchasing an insurance policy. If the loss or claim is already there, then it is too late to acquire insurance. Take out the policy before it is needed, then it is available when the disaster occurs.

Now let's shift gears and look at business structures that can aid you in protecting and preserving your assets. If you are not up-to-date with how to properly structure your business affairs, learn how it can cost you dearly.

CHAPTER EIGHT

Successful Business Structures

L ET'S START WITH THE BASICS. WHY DO YOU IN-
corporate or establish a limited liability company or partnership in the first place? Why not simplify matters and
conduct your business in your own name or as a d/b/a and file a
Schedule C attachment to your personal tax return? Wouldn't
this be easier, simpler and save you money? Surprisingly I have
seen too many accountants provide this simplistic advice to their
clients.

SEPARATE BUSINESS ENTITIES

The main reason to incorporate, or set up any other similar
separate entity from yourself for that matter, is to avoid per-

sonal liability. When you establish a separate corporate structure, and do business from that structure, it is that entity alone that is generally liable to the world, and not you, the corporate owner.

Of course, this assumes that you have met all of the legal formalities and other niceties, and you are not commingling personal and corporate assets. And too, it assumes that you are not undertaking personal guarantees as we discussed in Chapter Four. Tax benefits can be the sweetener to it all.

What this means is that you can still be the owner of the corporation, the sole director, and still be the president of the business. You make the decisions. You are the boss. You also work for the corporation as an employee. But, if there is a civil suit because one of the corporation's employees does damage to a customer's property or runs over a group of children while racing to the next job, the liability stops at the corporate level, not with you.

The claims in any such lawsuit are limited to the assets in the corporation. Your personal assets, however, are free from being attacked by the claimants. And with the creativity of plaintiff lawyers today, the potential claims against you are only left up to the imagination!

THE EXPOSURE

If, on the other hand, you were doing business without the benefit of incorporating, or other limited liability entity, and a civil suit was brought against the business, which is you, then each and every one of your personal assets are on the line. Everything you own is subject to the claims of your creditors. Your home, savings, personal property are all on the line. There is no way to protect and preserve your assets short of winning or settling the suit, and this alone can be costly to your pocketbook and reputation.

LIMITATIONS ON INSURANCE

Do you think that you are protected because you have insurance? Do you believe that by increasing your umbrella policy limits, your assets are protected? Think again.

What if the claim is an excluded claim and there is no coverage? And what if the insurance company is looking for ways to avoid making payment on the claim, and sets forth that you misrepresented yourself when you filled out the application in the

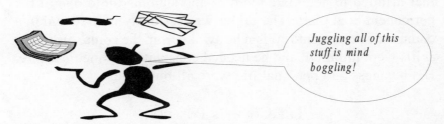

Juggling all of this stuff is mind boggling!

first place, and you have no coverage? Or, if when you reported the claim, you failed to properly give notice and there is no coverage. Remember that insurance companies are in the business of making money, not paying claims if they do not have to.

Take the example of an elderly couple named Howard & Millie. They worked long and hard for many years to build on this little dream spot on the waterfront. The dream started as a small boat marina and a restaurant with the finest home cooking you could find, and eventually became a popular and busy resort destination. In the summer, the boat slips were filled with boat owners spending their money on food and drinks in their restaurant and bar. And in the winter, this popular spot turned into a winter wonderland with the parking lots and yards filled with snowmobiles making the rounds.

They were now approaching the golden age with dreams of eventually selling the business and retiring. The business was not incorporated, but they carried sufficient insurance, so they thought.

One wintry January Sunday afternoon, a group of snowmobilers were cruising at top speed down the frozen river with plans of visiting Howard & Millie's resort. One of the snowmobiles quickly turned onto the property at such a high speed, that it failed to negotiate the turn and slammed into one of the permanent boat piers. The driver was seriously injured and in a coma for over a month. When he awoke from the coma, his motor skills were minimal, and he needed constant daily medical care. His business and personal life were all but gone.

THE COURT'S POSITION

Notwithstanding the fact that the snowmobiler's blood alcohol level was off the charts, he filed a several million dollar lawsuit in the District Court claiming that Howard and Millie had a duty to protect drunks, like this snowmobiler, that would come upon the property to visit, and that they failed to do so. A claim was filed with Howard and Millie's insurance company. The District Court refused to dismiss the suit and it was set for trial.

Almost up to the trial date, the insurance company was paying for all legal defense. The legal fees were expensive because the stakes were high. The first concern for Howard and Millie is that there was potential exposure to excess liability. The amount of the claim far exceeded the coverage limits. This meant that they would be personally on the line for all amounts above the policy limits.

With a strong, multimillion-dollar claim filed against them, and with much less insurance coverage amounts, this was not a very pleasant prospect for their retirement years.

But worse yet, just weeks before the trial was set to proceed, the insurance company filed for bankruptcy. And, the insurance company's high-priced downtown law firm, which Howard and Millie could not afford to pay, withdrew from the case. Now, all that Howard and Millie had worked for, their entire life dream, visions of retirement just around the corner, was no longer in focus.

Our office reluctantly took over the case. There was a tremendous amount of pressure on winning this suit, since everything was on the line. Nothing in between and no opportunity for settlement. Fortunately, we eventually succeeded on this case, but not without many sleepless nights, while this elderly couple agonized over their dilemma and paid dearly for it in many nonmonetary ways.

Protection from Personal Liability

The first level of protection that Howard and Millie could have had was a corporation. This may have protected them from personal liability. The second level would have been to have higher insured limits with a financially solid insurance carrier with broader coverage. They didn't, but fortunately they survived the ordeal, many others do not.

And certainly far more advanced levels of asset protection planning were available to them, had they only planned ahead.

THE C-CORP.

Remember, from a more technical standpoint, the different types of entities available to you. When you hear of a corporation, it could be a C-corporation or an S-corporation. The difference is primarily a tax issue. With the C-Corp, the corporation pays all taxes on profits. Above the shareholder's salary level, the profit distributions are again taxed (double taxation) on distribution.

THE S-CORP.

The S-Corp, on the other hand, simply passes through all profits or losses to the shareholders as would a partnership, taxing the profits only once. There are more restrictions on ownership of an S-Corp than a C-Corp, but they both provide the shareholders with the same protection from liability and creditor's claims.

A corporation is a separate taxing entity, taxed on its income. In addition to the regular corporate income tax, a corporation other than a qualifying corporation may be subject to the alternative minimum tax. Certain corporations, notably an S-Corp, may avoid tax by passing through all income and deductions to shareholders. An entity that is characterized as a corporation under state law must have specific corporate characteristics to be construed a corporation under the federal tax law.

An S-Corp is a pass-through entity that allows owners of closely held corporations to eliminate double taxation by passing through income, losses and credits to themselves without an intervening corporate tax. Taxable income is not taxed at the corporate level, but is passed through and taxed to the shareholders when there has been a distribution to them.

Similarly, corporate losses are deductible at the shareholder level to the extent of shareholder basis. A built-in gains tax and passive investment income tax may be imposed on S-Corps that have appreciation or retained earnings, and profits attributable to years in which they were regular corporations.

Partnership

A partnership is an entity, separate from its partners for tax purposes, but its income, loss, deductions, and other tax items are passed through to the partners. Whether an enterprise is a partnership, depends on the participants' intent, profit motive, degree of participation, the sharing of income and losses and documentation of arrangement. A partnership may be taxed as a corporation if it is publicly traded.

There are some new entities which are really a twist from other forms that have been around now for some time. Partnerships, general and limited, afford not only a type of liability protection, but also provide tax benefits depending on the type and structure. They can be used in a strict business setting or for

121

family asset protection planning structures as you will see in later chapters.

THE LLC

Limited Liability Companies (the "LLC") are a recent creature. The state of Wyoming first enacted by statutory provisions, this new entity which was more or less intended to have all of the liability protection of a corporation, and all of the tax benefits of a partnership. They have become very popular and most states have quickly enacted their own version of the LLC.

As the name "limited" implies, creditors cannot reach the assets of the owner members, as long as all of the formalities of the LLC are kept.

A LOOK AT ASSET PROTECTION USING AN LLC & A TRUST

In business and personal asset protection planning, many people wish to preserve and protect assets domestically, while maintaining income tax and economic neutrality. One way of doing this is through the combination of a "domestic asset protection trust" and an LLC, according to Jack Allgood, a CPA and tax partner with the firm of Levine, Hughes & Mithuen, Inc., Englewood, Colorado. This is one more example of using synergy to accomplish asset protection planning.

Let's say that you desire to sell your residence, purchase a replacement residence, roll over the gain and protect the equity you have established from creditors. First, you choose to establish an LLC to serve as a mortgage lender and an income tax-defective domestic trust (the Trust) to be the LLC's primary member.

You sell your primary residence for say $500,000, with a gain of $400,000 that is deferred under Internal Revenue Code Section 1034. The replacement residence is purchased from an independent third party for a fair market value of $1,400,000, using $400,000 as a down payment.

At the same time, you would transfer $1,000,000 to the Trust. Simultaneously, the Trust exchanges the $1,000,000 for a 99% membership interest in the newly formed LLC. The remaining 1% LLC membership interest is issued to a relative in exchange for cash. The LLC then serves as the mortgage lender to facilitate your purchase of the replacement residence.

Under the above scenario, according to Jack Allgood, you have shifted $1,000,000 to the Trust with a membership interest in the LLC. The Trust should provide for asset protection if managed properly. The Trust instrument must contain the powers to shift to offshore control if necessary, thus making it transferable for foreign supervision and administration. (More on the "control" issue in Chapters Ten, Fifteen & Sixteen).

According to Jack Allgood, you would recognize interest income passing through the grantor-type Trust from the LLC. This income recognition is offset by the deduction for mortgage interest paid by you. Economically, your cash position represents a payment to yourself. From a net worth analysis, the LLC membership is always equal to the mortgage indebtedness. On satisfaction of the indebtedness, a liquidating distribution can be made to you.

With the establishment of the LLC, according to Jack Allgood, capitalization of your membership interest is protected by most state's laws. The Trust manages the LLC, effectively giving you control. The LLC collects mortgage interest from you, incurring only a small deductible operating expense.

Additionally, there is a virtual alphabet soup of business entities, which also afford the advantage of limited liability.

THE LLP

For example, a relatively new form of legal structure called a Limited Liability Partnership ("LLP") is in essence a General Partnership, which was formed to confer limited liability on partners. If a business is conducted as a LLP, the partners will not be responsible for the debts and obligations of the general partnership.

LIMITED PARTNERSHIPS

A Limited Partnership ("LP") is a traditional form of organization. Under this method of doing business there exist one or more General Partners as well as a number of Limited Partners. The Limited Partner enjoys limited liability, but the General Partner does not.

Unless limited as a Limited Liability Partnership ("LLP"), the General Partners will have personal exposure for the partnership debt. Oftentimes the General Partner is a corporation which can limit the exposure of the General Partners, particularly if thought and consideration are afforded to the jurisdictions, and the General Partners are incorporated.

The LPA

A Limited Partnership Association ("LPA") is a somewhat unusual form of organization and is often employed where family members are invested together in a business venture. It is often employed in the arena of estate planning and has, as one of its hallmarks, the provision that its members have no right to withdraw. Unlike an LLC, where a member can contribute services in lieu of cash for membership ownership, LPA owners are restricted to cash or property contributions.

Other forms found in some states in the bowl of alphabet soup include Nonprofit Associations ("UNA"), Nonprofit Corporations ("NP"), and Cooperatives ("Co-op"), in which the use of each is somewhat different than the more traditional "for-profit" entities.

The Goal: Liability Protection

The key distinctions to any of the above different entities are the amount of liability protection you gain and the tax advantages of each. Which is right for you depends on your goals. But most importantly is that you do not exist in a day to day state of exposure which can be reduced significantly by conducting your business activity through a separate business entity. Simply filing the IRS Schedule C as a sole proprietor without the protection of business entity shield is inviting financial disaster.

No matter how large or small your business is, or whether it is full time or part time, you should always incorporate or use one of the other entities to protect and preserve your assets. Even if there are no tax benefits, which often there are, limit your exposure to the assets retained within the entity and don't have everything on the line for the next nut case you cross paths with.

USING MULTIPLE ENTITIES

And, if one entity is good, then are two or more entities better to help stay ahead in the race? Let's look at an excellent example of how using multiple entities in a business structure can be beneficial to you.

Mark Chuckly owned a very successful business. He started years ago repairing and selling pools and spas, which grew out of his small management company. Eventually the business grew to a full-scale sales team, with a large crew of servicemen and support staff. The fleet of vehicles numbered in the dozens.

The business continued to grow, and a sports and exercise equipment department was added to the operation. A new, large, modern facility was purchased and added on to accommodate the sparkling showrooms and accommodate the growing number of staff. Mark's success was truly a story based upon hard work and success over many years of dedication to customer service. The problem was that he had all of his assets under one entity, which left all of the assets exposed if any one of the segments of the business ran into a problem.

All of Mark's business and assets were held under one corporate shell. If there was a lawsuit due to a serviceman improperly installing or servicing a spa, then the entire fleet of vehicles, the management segment of the business, the swimming pool division, the health and exercise department, and the real estate which housed the different operations, would all be exposed to this liability. All of Mark's eggs were held in one basket.

DIVERSIFY BUSINESS STRUCTURES

A solution to protect and preserve Mark's diverse assets was relatively simple, and not so simple. First, separate limited liability companies and corporations were established for each individual segment of the business, with one corporate entity being the holding company for the others. The management function was placed under one entity known as XYZ Management; the profits and losses would pass through to the holding company. If there were any lawsuits against this entity, they stopped there.

Same with the pool and spa division, known as XYZ Spa and Pool, and the same with the XYZ Real Estate Company, with profits and losses passing through to the holding company, and importantly, the liability stopping at each entity. Of course, Mark and his wife were the sole shareholders of the S-Corp. holding company, and all benefits passed down and through to them.

Perhaps one of the more important decisions Mark made,

was to put the fleet of vehicles into a separate entity and lease them back to the service company; not only were profits and losses passed through and liability limited within this entity alone, but this afforded some great tax advantages with the leasing program which Mark's accountant eventually put into place. Everyone working closely with Mark's accountant to maximize tax advantages was essential.

You can see by looking at Mark's situation, an important example of the synergistic effect in action, but still working with one very basic tool of separate entities. The concept is simple. Putting the concept into action, and doing it now before trouble was at the doorstep, was the key. Mark was aggressive enough to take the necessary steps to protect his assets.

A separate entity for each of Mark's individual activities was designed to limit the liability within any one entity and not spill over into other business operations. The big national and international corporate names have been doing this for years, so why not do the same for your business?

TAX BENEFITS

In practice, dividing up the business operations is obviously not always so simple, since much creative tax work needs to accompany this new structuring, with added tax and accounting burdens every year. But, after all is said and done, the asset protection value is greatly enhanced by these multiple layers of protection.

Oftentimes, with good tax advice (remember these things work together), there is great opportunity for good tax advantages with multiple entities.

LIMITING PERSONAL GUARANTEES

And what is more, Mark had a habit in the past, as most owners of closely held businesses do, of giving that personal guarantee freely, so as to allow for expansion and growth of the business. The new structure provided a better argument to Mark's new lenders as to the multiple value.

Remember that the sum of the parts often exceeds the sum of the whole. He was able to better negotiate lender's demands for personal guarantees and even avoid them altogether in many situations. In this situation, the synergy multiplied itself even more so.

What could be more important for a business owner than to protect personal assets, preserve the assets within the company, have added tax advantages, and create a greater value using the synergy of basic ideas and concepts together? You will see that there are many more benefits in applying the concept of synergy as you proceed with this book. Look for them and see how you might apply them in your life.

I think I am starting to see the key to some of this stuff.

MULTIPLE BUSINESS OWNERS

Does it matter how you and your fellow shareholders own a business entity? Only everything in the world, if you are interested in asset protection planning and wealth preservation.

Let's start with the birth of a new high tech type business. Two or three individuals start with an idea that they are certain will succeed. Each has a resource or skill to contribute... money, experience, time, or whatever. The focus is on success and the game plan is to pull it together, including finding additional money. So what else is important?

Atwell Humbers was referred to my office from a good friend and client. He was about sixty years old and had been in business with two other partners for almost three decades. Atwell and the two others started a small electronic assembly operation in the garage at one of the partner's homes and shared the responsibilities based upon their expertise.

In only a few short years, they were operating out of a large manufacturing facility, volume was in the millions, office staff and assembly line employees continued to grow, and each of the three were pulling in large, comfortable, six figure salaries. They were best of friends, owned homes in the same upscale neighborhood, their wives entertained and traveled together on vacations, and everything was as close to utopia as one could get, until the big surprise for Atwell came.

Atwell quickly came to learn that just being a major shareholder and chief officer of his own company, provided little security and little asset protection.

130

Atwell arrived at the office one morning to discover his key would not open the front door. When Atwell finally gained entry from a secretary, he found that his plush, stylish office was packed up in boxes and crates, and he was being moved out. Of all the nerve! He was angry beyond description, as you can imagine. His other two partners of almost 30 years no longer had use

This time I am really madder than hell and ain't gonna take it no more!

for him, and found reasons to justify their actions. Maintenance of his standard of living and secure retirement for Atwell was now in question, at the very minimum. The other two partners were offering him a "comfortable" severance package. Atwell was outraged.

When I first meet with Atwell, he explained that he believed for all these years, there was no need for an Employer-Employee Agreement or a Stockholder's Buy-Sell Agreement, and he had neither. Things had worked well informally between the three of them for all these years, so why the extra paperwork?

EMPLOYMENT AGREEMENTS

As an owner of a corporation or other entity, unless you are in complete control of every aspect of the operation, you can be fired. Remember, in the eyes of the corporate structure, without an Employment Agreement like in Atwell's case, you are nothing more than an employee.

In most states across the country, employer and employee relationships are terminable at will by either party. The company can fire you or any other employee, with or without cause. Of course there are legal exceptions to this, but this is the general rule. It makes no difference that you have an ownership interest in the company.

So if other owners, or new owners, or a board of directors now believe that you are not carrying your own weight, or that new, younger, fresh blood would be more beneficial to the com-

But I wear all the hats... how can they survive without me?

Exit Plan

pany, you can be moved out the door. Like Atwell, your first line of defense would have been to have a written Employment Agreement. These have been given flashy names such as golden parachutes or severance agreements or others, but they all boil down to about the same thing.

What are the reasons that your employment can be terminated, and how you are compensated if that occurs? Without an Employment Agreement, like Atwell, you are at the mercy of others.

SHAREHOLDER BUY-SELL AGREEMENTS

And too, what good is it if Atwell was still one-third owner in a successful and profitable company. He might just as well have owned many shares of AT&T or IBM on the sideline and be unemployed. If and when there was a shareholder's distribution, of course, he would be provided for. But first, how much salary or expenses can be paid out to the other shareholders that controlled the checkbook? How much will be left over for him and his ownership?

A properly drafted Shareholder's Buy-Sell Agreement would have answered many of Atwell's other questions. Under what conditions could the company or other shareholders buy out Atwell? At what price? What were the formulas to be used to arrive at a fair price? How would the price be paid for? What about death of one of the partners…how can you avoid having the heirs, a spouse or children, now trying to run the business following death?

The above and many more issues are all the topic of a well-drafted Buy-Sell Agreement. Atwell had none.

LITIGATION

Because the stakes were very high for Atwell, with one-third interest in a multimillion dollar company, and partners pulling down very large six figure salaries and benefits, all stops had to be pulled.

We filed a shareholder's suit at once in court on his behalf. Expensive expert business valuators were brought in, along with financial planners for future dollar valuation. The attorney's fees, costs and expenses were enormous. Both sides were quickly posturing for the stronger position. All of this could have been avoided.

Eventually, a very handsome buyout and settlement was negotiated by our office for Atwell. He took a large amount of cash, some over time and some when the deal closed, real estate, and a great health and pension package. At times I wasn't sure that either he or his health would outlive the litigation and settlement, but he and his lovely wife are doing well today. I am convinced that others might not have done so well.

THINK & ACT

All of Atwell's issues should have been spelled out early on in the relationship, and updated as time necessitated it, so as to provide for Atwell or the other partners.

Ahhh, now I can wake up and smell the coffee.

Atwell's outcome was better than in many multi-owner business situations. Perhaps the worst scenario I've witnessed is when two individuals desire to go into a business as equal partners. What happens when there is a stalemate on decision making? Who is the tie breaker?

Too often, very successful businesses suffer because the equal partners cannot agree on a simple matter. Equal ownership should be avoided at all costs, or at a minimum, spell out how to deal with these issues in the Buy-Sell Agreement. There are some options, but none as good as avoiding two equal business owners in the first place.

Avoid Spousal Partners

Worthy of note is that it is not advisable to name spouses as officers or directors or co-shareholders when it is not necessary. Not only can this help prevent spouses being named in litigation, should shareholders or officers or directors be named in a suit, but also can avoid serious complications in the event of divorce. Keep in mind that single member owners, managers and officers are often named in litigation along with claims against a corporation, and even though later dismissed, it can be costly in both monetary and non-monetary terms.

And if you own a business, whether it be 10% or 100%, what have you done lately to see that your interests are preserved? If you pass on or suffer a disability, would the business survive? Would your heirs survive the business? Would the business survive them? What plans have you made for business succession if one of a dozen scenarios came your way?

For many business owners, their biggest asset is their business, yet they fail to take the steps to protect themselves from the possibilities. You must take the time and effort *now* to think through the possibilities, and look for solutions. If your doors are locked when you arrive tomorrow, or yesterday you suffered a disability, or worse a death, then it is much too late to act.

Today is the time to take the necessary steps using competent experienced legal, tax and financial planning counsel to help protect and preserve your business interests.

Now, let's look at how your choice of address might affect your asset protection planning. And, can you survive bankruptcy and creditor's rights without going broke? When times get really tough, these are important issues in wealth preservation.

CHAPTER NINE

Surviving the Financial Crisis

AVE YOU EVER THOUGHT THAT THE STATE YOU choose to reside in will make a difference in protecting or preserving your assets? Do you think that your state borders are only lines drawn on a map?

Well, think again. Just as certain states are "tax-havens" and do not tax certain or any income you earn (see Chapter Two for a list of these states), certain states offer better stateside asset protection planning than other states. Where you hang your hat makes all the difference as to how much of your assets you can protect.

Just like you will explore in the later Chapters in this Book under Section Three, which looks at offshore advantages for asset protection planning, there are different states in the U.S. which offer far greater benefits in protecting and preserving assets. Again, early planning is the key to success.

FINANCIAL SETBACKS

Let's face the facts. Not everyone's portfolio safely and consistently goes up and up, never having setbacks or cash flow problems. The reality is, that a sudden change in the economy can play havoc with long term investment plans. And, unplanned business challenges, or new irresistible opportunities, can throw you for a loop.

Even the best planners can, and will, experience financial setbacks. But the strong tend to survive over the long term. Many make money, fewer keep it. Generally, a hallmark of most successful people is that they have experienced more than one setback in their life on the path to financial success.

USING LEVERAGE

Before the Industrial Age, it was very unusual for an individual to owe money to more than one creditor. Multiple creditors simply did not exist. The laws over the centuries have changed so that debtors could no longer be forced into prison for unpaid debts. Then, slowly, laws were passed to allow an individual to start over again if he got too heavily into debt.

Today, you use credit and borrowed money to improve the quality of your life and move up the social and economic ladder. Sometimes this endeavor is wildly successful, and other times it is a disaster. Countless numbers of successful businesses, and great fortunes, have been made with borrowed money. Using credit is not a sign of a defective character, as it was once viewed.

By using leverage, it allows you to reach beyond your financial abilities to seize the dreams that might otherwise elude you. This is good business sense, as long as debt is used wisely and does not become a cash-flow trap.

You will recall in Chapter Four that Americans are taking on an unprecedented amount of debt for everyday basic living, often for no other reason than the economy has been strong and they are making a good income. And too, many small and medium sized businesses are expanding at rapid rates that simply cannot be sustained during a business slowdown. It all looks good when the economy is moving along at a growth pace, but what goes up must come down.

What happens if you cannot repay borrowed money or repay the interest amounts? At least thank goodness, you no longer need to worry about debtor's prison.

U.S. BANKRUPTCY

The framers of the U.S. Constitution in Article I gave Congress the power to establish uniform laws on the subject of bankruptcies throughout the United States. Discharge of debts began as early as 1841 and the first modern bankruptcy law was adopted in this country in 1898. Thereafter it was amended in 1938, again in 1978, 1984, and several subsequent occasions thereafter.

Keep in mind that the purpose of bankruptcy laws is to equally distribute a debtor's assets among his creditors. A secondary function is the collection of monies owed to him. All of this is generally accomplished without leaving a debtor with nowhere to live, or stripping away all of his assets.

The role of the Bankruptcy Court today is to resolve issues of outstanding claims and give the debtor a fresh start without past burdens. This is bankruptcy law.

LEVELING THE PLAYING FIELD

While creditors have rights, so do you, under a multitude of Federal and State Statutory provisions. For example, the *Fair Debt Collection Practices Act* regulates the activities of debt collectors, prohibiting certain practices entirely. The *Fair Credit Reporting Act* is designed to protect you against the dissemination by consumer reporting agencies of obsolete or incorrect information. The *Fair Credit Billing Act* protects you against unfair and inaccurate billing practices. The *Truth in Lending Act* requires a lender to state plainly the terms of repayment in language which is concise and uniform.

The *Equal Credit Opportunity Act* is intended to protect you from creditors that unfairly deal with you regarding your age, religion, race, sex, marital status, and national origin. Each of these Federal Laws, and an untold number of state laws, are designed to level the playing field, so that your creditors deal with you fairly and truthfully. If not, you have legal recourse against them.

Even the IRS has come under Congressional scrutiny to be kinder and gentler in dealing with you. The Taxpayer Bill of Rights has been greatly expanded, setting forth limits and conduct that the IRS is to follow. Congress has simply placed restrictions and continues to tighten the leash on the IRS on how aggressively it can collect taxes.

There are alternatives to filing bankruptcy and losing almost everything. Bankruptcy Chapters 7 and 13 (and in certain circumstances Chapters 11 & 12) offer a debtor the possibility of retaining certain property that was used to secure a loan. Mortgage lenders are given preferred status in a bankruptcy.

Most states permit a person filing bankruptcy to retain a part of home ownership. As you will see, this right in protecting your home, what is called "homestead rights", varies greatly from state to state so that your place of residence can become critical if you run into financial problems.

ALTERNATIVES TO BANKRUPTCY

Keep in mind that if you believe that you can repay your debts over three to five years and maintain a reasonable lifestyle, bankruptcy may not be the best for you. Simply trying to renegotiate a "work-out period" with your creditors may be the simplest and easiest solution. Remember, if you owe someone a little money, *you* have a problem; but if you owe your creditors lots of money, *they* have a problem.

See if there is a method for you to help them solve their

problem, as well as yours.

Try to get your creditors to settle for less. Initial contacts by telephone are often best. You can lay the framework for further discussions and feel out how they might respond. Keep an open line of communication and always be truthful. This doesn't mean that you need to wear your heart on your sleeve or give away your strategies, but if you want them to work with you, you must be credible and believable.

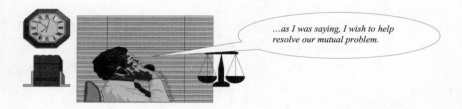

…as I was saying, I wish to help resolve our mutual problem.

Meeting with your creditors face to face, particularly your largest ones, is often essential. Explain how you have built a strong relationship with them in the past and how you look to further that relationship. Explain in simple terms what went wrong. Importantly, present them with a well-thought-out game plan as to how you intend to correct the situation, and why you believe you will succeed.

SELL YOURSELF

Most importantly, always negotiate from a position of strength. You must be in control, not them. Approach your creditor with a win-win situation. Convey the attitude that you can, and will, do whatever is necessary to meet your obligations, and that you are prepared to take any and all action to meet your commitments. And whatever you do, do not be derailed by the creditor that at first appears to refuse to make concessions about your obligations.

Your attitude should clearly convey confidence in your plan, even though you cannot presently meet your commitments. Explain how it is in the best interest of both parties to be cooperative and resolve matters together. Thoroughly review and explain how your plan will work, and how they will benefit. Be sure the creditor understands what it is you can do today, and what things will occur in the future. Be specific. At a minimum, make small commitments and keep them.

Seek Alternatives

Another suggestion is to solicit your creditor's advice. See what options they believe that they can assist you with. Local bankers and creditors in a community appreciate the honesty and opportunity to build long lasting relationships, and they will often respect you honestly soliciting their help. Don't whine. Demonstrate your abilities, and show them that you seek an opportunity to work with them and keep them part of your team.

Regardless of the lack of success during your first discussions with your lenders, be prepared to go back again and again. Always leave the door open. The creditor may have a change of heart when they see your persistence. Or better yet, if the lender eventually sees that they stand to gain more by cooperating with you, this may bring them around in due time. Express your disappointment on not resolving matters when you meet, but encourage further communications with them.

BANKRUPTCY PLANNING

If bankruptcy becomes the only way out, intelligent, advanced planning and competent legal counsel are essential for protecting and preserving your assets. The state and federal laws are there for your benefit. Do not be afraid to use them for their intended purposes.

And be prepared, if you do file bankruptcy, that you can, and oftentimes will, lose some of your investment property. And too, understand that bankruptcy will adversely affect your credit standing for several years to come. While you will not be required to wear the scarlet letter "B" on your chest, it will probably have more effect on you personally, than others who learn about it.

But if filing for bankruptcy becomes a necessary option to fend off the creditors, or if you are unable to pull together an agreeable strategic payback plan, then you must review the exemptions that are allowed in the state that you presently reside in and consider if moving to another state makes financial sense.

Anyone planning for bankruptcy with sizable amounts of assets should always consider relocating to another state which allows for greater amounts of exemptions under those state laws. The possibility of such a move should be contemplated as early as possible, if bankruptcy looms on the horizon.

STATE EXEMPTIONS

First, what are state "exemptions"? The answer is that each state permits certain categories of assets to be excluded, in part or in whole, from creditors during bankruptcy.

In other words, your creditors cannot attack certain assets. For example, most states exempt a portion of your wages from your creditors. This amount can vary from zero to one hundred percent. In certain states you can completely, or mostly, exempt the category of wages you receive from your creditors claims.

Disability Insurance and certain motor vehicles are generally in a class of assets that generally receive preference in your favor and not your creditors; personal household items and burial plots, and payments for health and life and accident insurance are generally excluded; and retirement plans, diamond rings (depending on size), tools, furniture, liquor permits, animals, and certain security deposits are other types of exemptions, depending on the state in which you file for bankruptcy.

Chapter Twenty Two compares the advantages and disadvantages of using stateside versus offshore insurance products to maximize your exemptions of insurance products. This is important for bankruptcy planning.

The list goes on and on, again depending on the state where you live. The list of exemptions vary so widely and greatly as to the types and amounts of assets that are excluded from your creditors, that a book on this topic alone could be written.

HOMESTEAD EXEMPTIONS

Even more significant is the difference in personal home exemptions that are allowed state by state. Because of this, it is not unusual to find families facing the prospect of filing bankruptcy to sell their home and moving to another state. They simply flee a state with little or no homestead exemption in favor of a state with substantially more generous homestead exemption laws.

Some states have no homestead exemptions at all. For example, Connecticut, Delaware, Maryland, New Jersey, Pennsylvania, Rhode Island and the District of Columbia (except condominium deposits) have no homestead exemption at the time of last inquiry. That means you have no protection for your home, often the largest asset, if you file for bankruptcy in any of those states.

States offering nominal homestead exemption (upon recent inquiry) are Alabama (160 acres to $5,000), Arkansas ($2,500 depending on option used), California (up to $45,000 depending on status and option), Colorado ($45,000), Georgia ($5,000), Hawaii ($20,000 or $30,000 depending on status), Idaho ($30,000), Illinois ($7,500), Indiana ($7,500), Kentucky ($5,000), Louisiana ($15,000), Maine ($7,500 or $60,000 depending on status), Michigan ($3,500), Mississippi ($30,000), Missouri ($8,000), Montana ($40,000), Nebraska ($10,000), New Hampshire ($5,000), New Mexico ($20,000), New York ($10,000), North Carolina ($7,500), Ohio ($5,000), Oklahoma (unlimited on ¼ acre or $5,000), Oregon (up to $20,000 depending on status), South Carolina ($5,000), Tennessee (up to $7,500), Utah (up to $10,000 for married couples plus $500 per independent), Vermont ($30,000), Virginia ($5,000), Washington ($30,000), West Virginia ($7,500), Wisconsin ($40,000), and the great state of Wyoming ($10,000).

States offering a better, but not the best homestead exemptions are Arizona ($100,000), Massachusetts (up to $200,000 depending on status), North Dakota ($80,000) and the glittering state of Nevada ($95,000).

States offering a more creative opportunity for placing large amounts of assets into a home and protecting them from creditors are Iowa (unlimited exemption amount for less than ½ acre within city and up to 40 acres in rural areas), Kansas (unlimited up to 1 acre within city or up to 160 acres in rural areas), Minnesota (unlimited for less than ½ acre within city or 160 acres in rural areas), and South Dakota (full exemption up to 1 acre within city or up to 160 acres in rural areas).

PARADISE?

Perhaps the two states offering the best opportunity to protect and preserve your assets are the states of Florida and Texas. This is particularly true, considering the value of homes and properties in many parts of these states. In other words, you have a reasonable degree of preserving your money placed in your home in these two states following the conclusion of your bankruptcy.

For example, in the Sunshine State of Florida, 100% of the value of your home located on up to ½ acre within a municipality is exempted, and 100% up to 160 acres in rural areas. What makes Florida more attractive than other states with similar exemptions is primarily the resale value of homes. The home prices are generally far greater in Florida than in other rural states, so you have far greater amounts of money that you can place into an existing or new home, and remove it later, following the bankruptcy.

Not to be outdone, in levels of grandeur, is the state of Texas. This state offers an unlimited homestead exemption if the home is located on up to 1 acre within a city, or 100 acres located elsewhere; and a family can exempt up to 200 acres outside of town. And importantly, the exemption can be retained if the property is rented to someone else, providing you do not purchase another homestead.

Considering the value of some of the ranches in Texas, and beachfront and other exclusive homes located in Florida, a huge amount of money can be stashed into a home in either of these two states, protecting and preserving for your benefit if you plan ahead for bankruptcy protection.

HOW PLANNING CAN WORK

In practice, does advanced bankruptcy planning really work? You bet it does!

The Wall Street Journal referred to the states of Florida and Texas as having become magnets for individuals filing for bankruptcy. One celebrity case included former Baseball Commissioner Bowie Kuhn who sold his New Jersey home for $1,000,000 and moved to Ponte Vedra Beach, Florida, just before his New York law firm went belly up (keep in mind that New Jersey has no homestead exemption!). Under New York law, Kuhn could have been held personally responsible for the debts of the partnership.

Another noteworthy celebrity was Marvin Warner of the failed Ohio-based Home State Savings Bank, who quickly sold his Ohio horse farm and purchased a 160 acre horse farm outside of Coral Gables, Florida, for $2,200,000. Taking full advantage of Florida laws, Mr. Warner was able to protect approximately $6,000,000 in assets from creditors when the bank failed, which compared to Ohio law where only $5,000 in homestead exemptions were available. And he was able to protect over $3,000,000 in cash by investing in annuities, a benefit he would not have attained in Ohio.

The Rules

What are the steps you must keep in mind if you see a hint of a calamity on the horizon? There are several basic rules to follow.

Plan Ahead

First, plan well in advance of filing for bankruptcy. There are clear bankruptcy laws that will "unwind" a transfer if done to defraud, hinder or delay your creditors. Fraudulent conveyances used to defraud your creditors by avoiding pre-established rights to your assets, must be avoided.

The more contemporaneous transfers are with filing for bankruptcy, obviously the more suspect your actions become. Taking action far enough in advance is always desirable, if not essential. Too often debtors wait until the last minute to react, and then it is often too late to do anything, except perhaps panic.

BE REASONABLE

Second, do not be too greedy. Taking aggressive steps to protect and preserve your assets often falls into questionable gray areas. If you are walking the fine line between what you can and cannot do, use great caution. If you are acting in good faith and do not become too greedy with assets, you may be able to finish a bankruptcy in far better shape than if you did nothing at all.

COMPETENT LEGAL ADVICE

Finally, get good competent legal advice and know the laws of the states that apply in your situation. You can do the same as Bowie Kuhn and Marvin Warner did by selling your home and moving. And then you can arrange your affairs far enough in advance of bankruptcy, so that you can maximize the amount of property claimed as exempt, therefore minimizing the amount subject to creditor's claims. This can be accomplished by converting your assets from nonexempt to exempt property, and using nonexempt property to pay off debts of exempt property.

The bankruptcy laws permit pre-bankruptcy planning and converting nonexempt status of property. Remember, the goal of the Bankruptcy Code is to allow you to get a fresh start. Following top-notch legal advice early on so you stay within the rules is essential. If a short term or long term financial crisis appears in your future, there are clearly opportunities to protect and preserve your assets.

Let's now look at how Family Limited Partnerships can provide tax benefits and asset protection. How can this tool help you fend off creditors? How can Family Limited Partnerships protect and preserve your assets for future generations while providing great tax advantages today? And importantly, how can this domestic asset protection tool be used aggressively in off-shore asset protection planning?

CHAPTER TEN

Family Limited Partnerships For Asset Protection Planning

I N EARLIER CHAPTERS, WE LOOKED AT DIFFERENT forms of company entities as vehicles to limit claims or judgments against your assets and keep creditors from reaching you personally. Let's now look at another type of entity, which is of great value for asset protection planning, and a tremendous tool for providing tax advantages.

FAMILY LIMITED PARTNERSHIPS

Take note closely to the form of a Family Limited Partnership, since we will return to this concept in the final chapters of this book. This, combined with other tools, creates the most advanced family asset protection planning technique available today in offshore planning.

Think for a moment about an asset planning structure that would allow you to park assets into it, and have a high degree of protection from future creditor's claims. Add to those benefits, an opportunity to generously exceed the maximum allowable amounts of gift giving to your heirs. And to make it even more desirable, how about if you could maintain use and control of those assets even after you created gift giving, and get paid a salary for managing those assets?

Sound like a formula too good to be true?

Enter Family Limited Partnerships. This is an important asset protection planning tool allowing all of the above, and more. In Chapter Eight we defined partnerships in a more traditional business sense, and compared various entities to one another, looking at how to use multiple entities for better stateside asset protection planning. Now you can see how to use this same basic structure for more aggressive asset protection planning and reap tax benefits at the same time.

You've probably heard of Limited Partnerships, and perhaps even invested in a few. You write your check for perhaps $10,000 or $20,000 per share and receive a certificate stating that you own an interest in the Partnership. You generally have no voice or control in what happens, leaving all decisions to the General Partner.

Then, if and when there are profits from the Partnership's business and it is distributed to the Limited Partners, you receive your share. As the Limited Partner you have no liability beyond your investment. You just sit and wait for the profits to come in. At least this is how they are supposed to work.

FLEXIBLE PLANNING TOOL

Limited Partnerships have been used for many different types of business ventures over the years. I have personally been involved with the legal aspects of partnerships used for real estate investing into microbrewery pubs and other unusual businesses. Some are profitable for the Limited Partners, many are not. Too often the only ones that make any money are the General Partners in the form of commissions, fees, and guaranteed payments, with little profit left over for the Limited Partners. Some, on the other hand, have gone quite well.

The technical structure for a Family Limited Partnership ("FLP") is not much different from the ones you are probably familiar with. However, the big difference is that you, as the General Partner, can control, manage and use your assets in the limited partnership, and you are the one getting paid to manage the assets.

THE BASICS

Here is how it works. You place certain assets into Smith FLP. Consider it your nest egg. Then you become the General

155

Partner ("GP") owning a 1% interest in the limited partnership. This allows you to exercise all control over the assets. For now you also set yourself up as the Limited Partner ("LP") owning a 99% interest as well. This is a separate legal entity with tax reporting requirements. (In Section Three you will see another important method to holding this 99% interest in offshore planning.)

You:

Family Ltd. Partnership:

GP = 1% = Control

LP = 99%

ASSET TYPES

First, the type of asset you place into the FLP is generally the type that does not have tax benefits that you wish to preserve. For example, C-Corp stocks, money market funds, cash savings, notes, receivables, and similar assets are best to fund this entity.

You can place certain real estate into the account, but you might lose the tax advantages since they may not pass through to you. If you prefer, keep the money right where you have it today; you are just transferring the title to the assets into the partnership name. If properly done, these transfers are incomplete gifts for tax purposes, since they are actually for estate planning purposes.

If you can, avoid placing LLC membership interests, S-Corp stock, your personal residence, and investment real estate (which have tax advantages) into the partnership, since you may lose the tax advantages.

TECHNICAL ISSUES

For the more technically minded, there has been some debate in tax circles as to whether or not it is necessary or desirable to limit the type of assets you transfer into the Family Limited Partnership, and directing certain assets into a Trust instead.

The technical argument is that the partnership is merely a pass-through entity for tax purposes and will pass-through a Grantor Trust to you, the beneficiary anyway. (More on this Trust structure later in Section Three when you see how moving offshore can be extremely beneficial for more aggressive asset protection planning). However, I generally recommend the more conservative route.

The specific technical reasons are that pursuant to Code Section 1361(b)(1)(B), only a natural person or a Grantor Trust may be a holder of S-Corp. stock, and a partnership is not a permissible entity. And, under Tres. Reg. Section 1.1244(a)-1(b), an individual is not allowed to personally deduct losses, unless the individual or partnership entity was the original issuee; therefore this would preclude subsequent transfers to a domestic partnership if the partnership was not the original issuee.

In Rev. Rul. 85-13, the IRS takes the position that the owner of the Grantor Trust is treated as the owner of the Trust for tax

157

purposes, therefore when Code Section 1244 stock is transferred into the Trust, there is no transfer for tax purposes.

And in reference to Tax Deferred Annuities, under Code Section 72(u), only a natural person or a Grantor Trust is entitled to tax deferred treatment to an annuity.

Another technical point of reference that is critical, pertains to personal residences and second homes. It is uncertain whether a partner of a Family Limited Partnership may deduct mortgage interest under Code Section 163(h)(3). The language is inconclusive and could lead to the conclusion that only an individual or a Grantor Trust could deduct such interest. Similarly, it is also inconclusive if the current $500,000 exclusion of gain from the sale of residences under Code Section 121 would apply if a literal interpretation was taken.

For the same reasons set forth above, it is inconclusive if second home mortgage interest deductions would qualify if held by a partnership under Code Section 163(h)(3). As a result, both personal residences and second homes are best held in a grantor type Trust since the IRS takes the position that the owner of the Trust is treated as the owner of the Trust property for all income tax purposes.

SINGLE MEMBER LLC

You should also be aware that perhaps another good structure in which to hold a personal or second residence is a single member limited liability company, the single member owner being the Grantor Trust. While the Code and IRS position has not been clearly spelled out as of this writing, I have received

158

several tax opinions from qualified experts that take the position that this is solid tax planning and you, the owner of the Trust, can receive all tax benefits when the property is held in the single member limited liability company. However, this position is presently being argued in some tax circles.

The World of Uncertainty

Enough technical mumbo jumbo. As you can see, the world of taxes is oftentimes very unclear, providing all the more reason for obtaining second and third opinions from good qualified tax experts as discussed in Chapter Two. Reasonable people will disagree reasonably, and others simply have little or no knowledge of a certain area and will be afraid to admit it.

Managing the FLP

Now that the FLP structure is funded with assets, what do you do with them? The answer is to manage them for profitability. You, as General Partner, make the decisions as you did before. You can decide to move them around or change their nature, all in the partnership name. Instead of signing checks to draw from an account in your personal name, you now add "General Partner" after your name.

And, as General Partner you can pay yourself a guaranteed payment (a salary). The salary can be in the amount you reasonably see fit for the purpose of your function. And distributions can be made to the Limited Partners, of which you presently own 99%, as you determine necessary. Of course any income on the assets which is distributed is done so and taxed at the individual partner's tax rate. Compare that with the often higher tax bracket of 39.6% of an irrevocable trust, once income is over $7,900.00.

FLP & ASSET PROTECTION

What about the asset protection aspect? If, in the future, a creditor comes along with a claim against you, as a partner, the creditor cannot generally pierce a properly structured limited partnership and get to the assets. The creditor, armed with a Charging Order, can only lay claim to any distributions made to a partner. Therefore, if the General Partner, you, decide not to make any distributions to that partner, there is no money for the creditor to get their hands on.

Combine that feature with the fact that a creditor with a Charging Order may also be taxed with partnership income, even if he does not receive one single penny from the partnership (Revenue Ruling 77-137, 1977-1 C.B. 178, G.C.M. 36960 (Dec. 1976) and Evans v. Comm'r 447 F.2d 547 (7th Cir. 1971)).

In other words, the mere fact a creditor obtains a Charging Order against the partnership gives rise to a tax obligation to the creditor. This may indeed encourage a creditor to settle for far less than the claim. This is a tremendous way to protect the assets and the income flow of your nest egg.

The Correct State

However, one caveat is necessary. Establishing a Family Limited Partnership in the correct state is critical. Depending on the state that the FLP is established, some states have expanded creditor's rights against these structures, allowing creditors the additional remedy of selling the member's interest in a judicial foreclosure sale. Under this scenario, a third party might end up purchasing the membership interest, and usually at a discounted price.

If you do not set up the Family Limited Partnership in the correct state, you could be faced not only with a creditor with a Charging Order, but also having to deal with a third party from whom you must repurchase the membership interest. Choice of states when selecting where to establish your Family Limited Partnership is essential, but when properly chosen, provides significant asset preservation. Colorado is generally one of the better states.

Gift Tax Benefits

And let us not forget about the gift tax benefits of a Family Limited Partnership.

This tool is another approach to pass valuable property to your heirs. As you are aware, you can presently gift $10,000 each year, tax free, to any one of a number of your heirs, with a combined spousal election totaling $20,000. Each year, you and your spouse can gift away Limited Partnership's interest as a tax-free gift. However, you are allowed to transfer the Limited Partnership interests at a discount to face value.

The theory is that these interests are not readily marketable, so you can adjust, or take a minority discount, and value accordingly.

It is the possibility of huge tax breaks using minority discounts that make these vehicles so popular to many searching for tax benefits. Because the Limited Partners have no control over the partnership assets, the value of those assets is decreased. Recent court rulings have upheld limited partnership discounting to 45%, although some very aggressive planners have found creative ways to take discounts as high as 60%. That works out to a tremendous tax savings in estate and gift taxes.

How Gifting Works

For example, a $1,200,000 portfolio in the limited partnership discounted at only 40% would mean that the assets would be valued at only $720,000. This is approximately the amount that can pass free of Federal Estate Taxes, depending on the tax year due to the current adjustment through 2006. And applying this same conservative discount, you could also gift away $28,000 per couple, to each of your children, every year, instead of only $20,000, without triggering gift taxes.

Year after year, this adds up to a very handsome tax savings. Compound the tax savings with the growth of those assets in the name of your children in their generally lower tax brackets, and you have saved a bundle in estate taxes.

Drawn by the possibility of such generous tax benefits, wealthy taxpayers and their advisers are always searching for new and creative uses for the Family Limited Partnership. Later in this book, you will see an even more creative example using this important tool. Remember the synergy!

Keep in mind that it is important to have an underlying business purpose for the limited partnership other than just tax avoidance. Even with this legal requirement, partnerships are still being used to hold family stock and cash portfolios, life insurance, and even investments made for minor children.

Practical Applications

The uses are endless. If you desire to take a step forward in the category of asset protection planning, this is an important and worthwhile step indeed. If you are in a high risk profession, or simply concerned about litigious clients or patients, this is an ideal vehicle in the right direction. As one example, you could place an office building where you conduct your profession into a Family Limited Partnership, leasing it back to your business or practice, and keep it out of reach of claims.

Or, subject to potential personal tax limitations discussed above, you could place your stock portfolio or cash savings into a Family Limited Partnership, keeping it out of reach of claims. In either of the above examples, you can continue to use the assets and pay yourself a fee or salary for doing so, while you provide gift giving to your children.

The wealthy parents of the "useless ski bum" might opt for a Family Limited Partnership due to concerns of assets being squandered away. You retain all of the benefits of use and control, and don't have to worry about your ski bum having access to spending their inheritance away on foolish pursuits. And re-

163

member, if the child gets into trouble, the creditors would generally only have a Charging Order, which means they could not get to the assets of the partnership, and would only have a right to any distributions, if and when made.

MULTIPLE FLPS

If one Family Limited Partnership is good, is two not better? In applying another example of the concept of synergy, if you wish to limit the exposure of a high-risk asset against low-risk assets, then using multiple limited partnerships is for you. For example, higher risk real estate could be placed into one vehicle and low risk cash in another. Then if someone slips and falls at your second home, only the real estate is subject to the claim, not the cash.

Remember that the Charging Order applies against your personal creditors, but those dealing with an asset within the partnership could still have recourse against that asset directly. Avoid commingling high risk and low risk assets together, and keep in mind possible tax consequences associated with this example.

PROPER PLANNING

These structures are constantly under IRS scrutiny and must be properly prepared and implemented. Even though the IRS conceded in 1993 that minority discounts could be applied to gifts to family members, the IRS is constantly rethinking its strategy. The big question is how these discounts are applied to gifts.

Paperwork must be carefully drawn. Having property professionally appraised by independent third parties for aggressive discounting is essential. And tax returns must be prepared every year. Notwithstanding these extra requirements, Family Limited Partnerships are still well worth the extra effort.

THINKING AHEAD

One hint about using Family Limited Partnerships in a most aggressive multiple structure: what might you do with the Limited Partnership 99% interest other than placing it in your name or the name of your children? What other entity might you control or use that could hold these interests for you to offer you even better family asset protection planning?

Later chapters will reveal this marvelous, aggressive tool used in conjunction with other tools, as the most advanced asset protection planning technique available today.

Yes I can see it clearly now Watson.

If you somehow think that you are immune from problems falling your way, think again. There are simply some things in life that are unavoidable. How you plan and act will make a big difference. But you must act today and set these tools in place before a calamity strikes.

SUMMARY OF BASIC ASSET PROTECTION PLANNING

Before we move on to the next, or second, segment of asset protection planning, which is the first small step in offshore planning, let's summarize the basic stateside tools that you have explored so far. Keep in mind that you will see in the third section how some of the basic stateside tools in the first and second segment will be used together to create some of the most aggressive, legal asset protection planning tools available to you.

Your Money, Your Choice:

First and foremost, you will recall that the basic premise of this book is that it is your choice and legal right to do with your money and property what you desire, as long as you are not defrauding or interfering with the rights or claims of someone else. Spend them, gift them away, invest them wisely, or legally and aggressively preserve them for you and your family's future use. It is entirely up to you. It is your money and property, so make your choice. But do it right, and do it legally.

Act Now:

It is your choice to implement a plan *today* if you desire to preserve a nest egg for the future and protect it from the jaws of plaintiff hungry sharks and lawyers. I emphasize the word *today*, since planning is one of the most critical elements of a well-implemented asset protection strategy. Waiting until some future date is often too late.

When the seas are calm is the time to take action. You cannot wait to buy a life raft when the boat is already starting to sink. Plan B requires that you act well in advance, just in case your Master Plan takes on water. Now, not later is the key! When the sharks surface for your blood, there is not much you can do.

Maximize Tax Savings:

You work hard for your money. Why pay more in taxes than you are legally obligated to pay? Most hard working folks just do not stop and think of the overwhelming amount of taxes that they really pay. There are income taxes, social security taxes, sales taxes, property taxes, excise taxes, gasoline taxes, sin taxes, corporate taxes, death taxes and many, many hidden taxes beyond our imagination.

The government is forever creating new strategies to help part you and your money from one another. The first way to preserve your hard-earned money is to seek out the very best tax

167

advice available and use it, and not be afraid to obtain second tax opinions.

Discourage Lawsuits:

Discouraging lawsuits is such a common sense basic tool of asset preservation that it is almost shameful to add this to the list. Unfortunately, and too often, a big ego gets in the way, wasting considerable time and money, and exposing hard earned assets to predators. Seek out the higher road. Take that extra initiative to try and resolve conflicts. Try even harder to avoid them in the first place by using good, complete documentation for the transaction and by seeking to avoid personality conflicts where you can.

Don't be willing to turn important financial decisions in your life over to a judge or jury who knows nothing about you or your life. Hard-earned money and property is too often lost by not avoiding litigation in the first place. If you are forced to litigate, but only as a last resort and when all else fails, then give 'em hell and let the word be known that you are a fighter!

Avoid Personal Guarantees and Unnecessary Debt:

To many it sounds overly simplistic: avoid personal guarantees and use debt wisely for solid investment purposes. Avoiding personal guarantees, or limiting them to the greatest extent possible, is generally easier than you might think. If your business venture fails, don't place at risk everything else in the world you own. Seek out the opportunities that permit you to avoid or limit personal guarantees at all times. And, when the economy turns, avoiding personal guarantees and unnecessary debt can mean the difference of your survival.

Formalize Personal Relationships:

Moreover, there are two opposite and extreme sides, both irrational, to love and breaking up. If not you, I am certain that you have witnessed friends of yours, men and woman, that conduct their personal affairs in an unquantifiable and unpredictable manner when in love or upon a falling out of love. Their actions might be characterized as simply stupid. Entering into a written agreement when cohabitating with another, when sharing a common law marriage, or prenuptial agreements before entering into marriage, at a time when common sense prevails, is the best protection to preserving your assets. Do not worry, you will still have things to argue about anyway.

Control Property Ownership:

Along the same lines as formalizing personal relationships, owning property together has certain special legal aspects that must be observed. Married couples should consider options other than joint tenancy, for example, tenancy by the entireties, where it is available. This tool has the potential of greatly expanding your homestead exemption and avoiding creditor's claims against the marital home. And too, agreements between non-married persons when owning property together should set forth the rights and obligations of each regarding the property, especially including when and how to sell the property.

Plan Ahead for Elderly Care:

Our elderly family members bring a special challenge in dealing with asset protection planning. As productive members of society for many years, they have contributed into the system. Notwithstanding this fact, Congress has taken great inroads to limit what they can now take out when they reach the twilight years of their life. Qualifying for Medicaid is a very complex and controversial issue to many. Regardless of where you stand, there are still legal measures that you or your elderly family members can take to help preserve a lifetime of assets for the next generation. They can still obtain benefits from a system that they have contributed long and hard into, if done legally and with sufficient advance planning. Caution is the key word here.

Organize Your Business Structure:

We have learned the importance of conducting our business affairs in an entity unique and distinct from our own person. When a separate business structure is properly set up and the ongoing formalities are met, you can limit your exposure to a lawsuit or business failure to that entity, and your personal assets cannot be touched. Beyond the basics, creative structuring of multiple entities can reap tremendous benefits from the asset protection standpoint, and with top-notch tax advice, yield tax savings as well. And importantly, when there is more than one business owner, having a well-thought-out agreement between partners to cover buy-out arrangements and employment issues is of utmost importance.

How to Survive the Crisis:

If a business failure seems inevitable, how you deal with the situation is critical. Attempting to amicably work out a financial problem with your creditors in good faith, is the first step that can often result in great benefits. A well-organized and implemented plan is critical. But if bankruptcy is inevitable, then this too must be thought-out and orchestrated well in advance to your benefit. How you design a bankruptcy plan and where you live when you file for bankruptcy can make the difference between going broke or preserving your assets.

Family Limited Partnerships Can Save Taxes and Preserve Assets:

Chapter Ten of the first section of this book introduced you to the Family Limited Partnership Agreement for tax and asset protection planning purposes. This vehicle has been around a long time and, when used properly, is a great planning tool. You will witness first hand, in the third and final segment of the book, how this structure can be used in one of the most aggressive forms of asset protection and wealth preservation planning. This tool, used by the very wealthy, and used together with other legal techniques, can undoubtedly help create a solid fortress around your assets as you will see in the Section Three on offshore planning.

Remember the Importance of Using Legal Tools Together:

Finally, synergy. If there is nothing else that you learn from taking the time to read this book, it is the concept of creatively combining different legal tools together for your own customized asset protection plan, to bring about the maximum benefits available to you.

With a little imagination on your part, you can structure a

171

well-defined plan that will help protect your money and property for later years, for you and your family, for when you need it most.

You Must Act Now:

Even with the best synergy in the world, if you fail to take action today, *now,* it may do you little good when you need it most. Taking affirmative action *today* and implementing that plan *now* is perhaps one of the most critical steps of your life if you truly and honestly desire to protect and preserve your hard earned assets.

Let us now move on to seeing how you can protect yourself and your family from natural disasters of death and disability when they knock at your door. These stateside measures actually can become incorporated into much more aggressive offshore asset protection planning as you will see in Section Three of the book. For now, you should be familiar with some of the concepts stateside; later we'll deal with how these critical tools can be incorporated into offshore planning.

The consequences following in Section Two, are a natural part of living, and no doubt you will be confronted with some of these issues during your lifetime.

****

SECTION TWO:

PROTECTING AND PRESERVING YOUR ASSETS FROM NATURAL DISASTERS

(STATESIDE & OFFSHORE PLANNING)

CHAPTER ELEVEN

Death & Wealth Preservation

E VERYONE, PARTICULARLY IN THE MOUNTAIN
paradise of Vail, Colorado where I choose to spend my
life, hopes that they will live forever long and healthy,
avoiding the burdens that come with getting older. The typical
lifestyle is to eat healthy and exercise but unfortunately, the inevitable occurs. Illnesses, disabilities, and death are part of getting older.

LIVING FOREVER?

If you are not concerned about what happens to your assets
after you die, then I invite you to skip ahead to the third and
final segment of this book, to look at what I believe is the most

aggressive type of asset protection planning, using offshore structures for the very serious, high asset, high income individuals.

I believe that Section Three, Advanced Asset Protection Planning (Moving Offshore) for the serious individual, is the most exciting part of wealth preservation planning available today. This is where you have an opportunity to set-aside from the sharks and other predators your money and property and have a high degree of confidence that it will be there available for you or your family.

Legally, there are no better asset protection planning and wealth preservation tchniques available today than you will explore in Section Three.

For the rest of us, understanding that death is a natural part of living, the importance of having a well-drafted and properly structured estate plan is essential to wealth preservation.

Importantly, a well-thought-out estate plan includes provisions not only for death, but also for disabilities. My friends in the insurance business tell me that middle-aged folks, perhaps like you and me, have ten times higher likelihood of suffering a disability than dying during this age category. The disability can be long or short term, and strikes many more than you can imagine. Disabilities is covered in Chapter Twelve.

INTEGRATED ASSET PROTECTION PLANNING

Most importantly, keep in mind that the asset protection tools we discuss in Section Two, concerning Wills and Trust, Durable Powers of Attorney, Irrevocable Life Insurance Trusts, and gifting, while common and typical in US stateside asset preservation, can and should be fully integrated into offshore asset protection planning techniques.

Actually, solid offshore asset protection plans incorporate stateside estate planning wealth preservation into the overall offshore plan. Planning only stateside or only offshore is missing the big picture.

First, let's look at the guidelines for a successfully implemented stateside estate plan, which will help protect and preserve your family's assets after your death.

Why estate planning in the first place? How does this fall into the category of asset protection planning and wealth preservation? Simple. Without direction from you of how and where you wish your assets to go after you die, the laws of the state you reside in will dictate those decisions for you. In most situations, this distribution will go to people you care little about, or who care little of you, and at great cost and expense to those you care about most.

Who Gets What?

The worst case scenario is that the state or federal government will get all, or most of what you worked years to accumulate. The heirs of your estate could be known as your state or federal government, completely excluding anyone or everyone else you desire. This is the basic law of descent and distribution, which comes into play if you fail to properly leave an estate plan behind after you die.

If, instead, you desire to protect and preserve your hard earned assets from the hands of those least desired, or at least for those of your choosing, putting in place a Will and Living Trust is essential. This is only the starting point for a good basic estate plan.

Keep in mind that it is important that you take an active role in your personal estate plan. You need to keep up on changes by reading and asking questions as to how new rules apply to you. While there are a number of constants in the world of estate planning, the tax code rules and applications are fluid and in continual change.

Remember that there are certain provisions that you can add to your estate plan that can mean the difference of incurring large estate tax burdens and other expenses in administrating your estate, or preserving the assets for your family.

Avoiding Taxes

Next, understand that your estate plan should address the concerns of potentially huge estate taxes that may be assessed upon the transfer of your assets when you die. The good news is that you can substantially reduce your estate taxes if allowable credits and proper estate planning techniques are used effectively.

It is essential that your various estate planners and advisers work closely together to legally reduce your taxable estate. There are both federal and state guidelines that must be closely followed. Moreover, you must prepare your estate plan, step by step, preparing a current financial statement of all assets and their values, relying upon qualified individuals to assist you in establishing and realizing your goals.

Have you identified financial objectives for your family and assets to be followed after your death? What are you waiting for?

THINK FAMILY

Finally, while your estate plan concerns property, more importantly it involves the lives of family and friends. You must think in terms of people, not just dollars and cents. What are the objectives and work ethics, values and self-reliance that you desire to instill in children? What are financial abilities of family members and loved ones as to managing the estate you leave behind? How will the plan actually work, day by day, when you are gone?

The relationships amongst family members and the function of the family unit as a whole must be thought out for a successful estate plan. In a simpler world, long established conflicts or sibling rivalry would not exist. But whoever said families are simple? Almost 500 years ago, the French essayist Montaigne made the enduring observation that *"There is scarcely any less bother in the running of a family than in that of an entire state."*

181

Up close, a family unit has many issues that need to be addressed.

CONSULTING WITH THE PROS

The above are all questions that you must ask your estate planning professionals **before** you retain them. At a seminar, the talk all might sound good. But in private, you need to talk one on one about specifically accomplishing your goals. And frank talk includes the fees and expenses to bring about your plan. Begin by listing the issues that are important to you on a piece of paper so you can remember what to ask.

Good intentions are only the beginning. You must collect your financial and personal facts and documentation, and share these with your planners, to bring about the best plan to protect and preserve your hard-earned assets.

Remember that good estate planning consists of both proper documentation and implementation. One without the other is not enough. A good estate plan includes the re-titling of assets, transferring ownership of assets, renaming beneficiaries of life insurance and retirement benefits, and many, many other details that must be taken into account.

The list of techniques for estate tax savings tools is a long one. But too often I have seen a high asset client walk into my office without even the basic organized estate plan to really assist with asset preservation, even though there exists a Will and a Trust. Often a long time attorney-friend helped put together their estate plan and it was assumed they had their house in order in the event of untimely death. Is death ever timely?

When Death Strikes

I remember Tom & Lindsay Burner, in their 40's, who had inquired on and off over the years about setting up a proper estate plan. Lindsay had been ill over a period of two years. They continued to postpone their estate plan until I finally urged them to sit down and get matters resolved, as a year end goal.

A Trust with Will and Durable Powers of Attorney and Dying Declaration for each was prepared and executed the week before Christmas, at a time when Lindsay was in better health. It was then only two days into the New Year, that she suddenly took a drastic turn for the worse, and she passed away the following day. It was very difficult for Tom and his three young daughters to accept her death, but at least they took solace in knowing that they had taken the correct steps for proper estate planning, saving a significant amount in estate taxes and establishing a legacy for the three girls.

Avoiding Family Conflicts

When death occurs, the creative and emotional opportunities for, and frequency of disputes among the friends and family members never ceases to amaze me. I recall only so well what became called the "Stradivarius Violin case", which I handled as a young attorney, only several years out of law school.

Mr. Nedley, a retired and widowed businessman, lived the final years of his life, as most would describe, as a packrat. Walking from one end of the huge comfortable home to the other was like walking through a maze. Old dusty boxes were piled up high, filled with possessions acquired over many years. While some of the boxes held no commercial value, some contained treasures which were worth a small king's ransom.

Half of the family was convinced that Mr. Nedley owned a violin collection, including a valuable Stradivarius, worth a sizable fortune. The other half of the family claimed that was nonsense and that the first group was just trying to leverage for more than their allotted share of the estate. The two groups and their attorneys filled the courtroom, on opposite sides, to argue their positions before the judge.

The judge burdened with the claims of the group alleging the existence of the rare and expensive violins did what any good judge would do. He directed the representative of the estate to hire expensive investigators and appraisers to get to the bottom of the violin issue. Month after month, well into the second year, inquiries were made with friends and families of the deceased Nedley to try and determine what happened, if anything at all, to the rare violins.

The local press picked up the violin issue. Mr. Nedley's personal and private lifestyle now became part of the community gossip. What was once a personal and private affair, was open to the world. The whole affair made a laughing-stock of the fam-

184

ily, considering the reclusive lifestyle Mr. Nedley lived. Nothing was private, and his matters were an open book for all to see.

The truth eventually came out after almost two years of huge legal, investigative, and appraisal costs and fees. There were no violins other than some beat up old instruments that hardly could fit the category of collectibles. The group alleging the existence of a Stradivarius collection had a creative, and perhaps hopeful, imagination. Arguing that an expensive violin collection existed also provided them with some perceived leverage of increasing their share of the overall inheritance. Neither side won in this ordeal, since the price of getting to the truth, and the breach to Mr. Nedley's privacy, was high. Needless to say the family members were no longer talking.

PLANNING GOALS

What are some of the goals you seek in proper estate planning?

Privacy is often one of them. Discouraging litigation, or family disputes is another. And too, preserving the assets from fees and costs, as well as estate taxes, are other important objectives. To the extent that you can accomplish each of these goals, you are better able to protect and preserve your assets for your family after you die.

Mr. Nedley could have easily added a provision in his Will or Trust that set forth that if anyone disputed or sought to contest the dispositive provisions, they would have been excluded altogether. In other words, he could have stated that if you do not like what you get and complain about anything, you lose everything. Placing anti-contest provisions in a Will or Trust is very important to help avoid family disputes after you are gone. This helps speed up the process and keeps the emotions from flaring up.

ANTI-CONTEST PROVISIONS

In a related case, I remember my client Mr. Eddon placed anti-contest provisions in his Trust. There were nine children left behind from two different marriages. Over the years the adult stepchildren never got over the hostility between themselves with their father leaving one wife for another and raising a second family. There was money, not a great amount, but enough to argue about.

His Trust clearly stated that if anyone disputed any provision in the Trust, that that person would lose their bequest. While there were certainly rumblings between some of the adult stepchildren after Mr. Eddon died, it quickly disappeared when the anti-contest provision was disclosed and they discovered that they might get nothing if they disagreed with their share amount.

AVOIDING PROBATE

Avoiding probate is often another major goal when you die. What is probate anyway? This is the legal process of passing title from the deceased to an heir or beneficiary after the death of the property owner. This is achieved by virtue of a judge or magistrate issuing an order of court providing legal authority to a third party, usually called the executor or representative, so that legal title can pass and become vested in the recipients, the heirs.

Preserve Assets

Probate costs money. Large legal fees and expenses are the norm when proceeding through probate. And it takes time.

Privacy

Perhaps the worst part of it all is that every single piece of your personal financial information becomes public. And too, you are paying big time for this breach of your privacy. There is simply no privacy during the probate process and it can quickly erode away your estate with the legal fees and expenses.

The objectives of proper estate planning are to avoid probate to save money and protect your privacy. This can best be accomplished by establishing a proper Will and Living Trust with provisions setting forth your wishes and goals to preserve your assets, as you desire. The dispositive provisions in the Trust are followed in private, and not in a public forum like a Will.

Two of the big differences between a Will versus a Living Trust are cost savings and privacy when you die. Undoubtedly, disposing of assets through a Trust is far superior to a Will in almost every situation.

Living Trusts & Pour-Over Wills

A Living Trust must still be used with what is called a Pour-Over Will. Even the most organized of individuals fail to keep each and every asset in the name of the Trust, generally owning some assets in their own name. When you die, those assets held in your name, instead of in the name of the Trust, "pour-over" into the Trust and will be distributed according to the terms of the Trust. Remember that the Pour-Over Will must still be administered by a Probate Court proceeding, but this should be nominal if you have your assets in the name of the Trust.

BASIC ESTATE PLANNING

Too often, a husband and wife are misled by improper advice to take jointly owned property in joint tenancy with rights of survivorship. The argument is simply that when ones dies, the other takes all and this simplifies your estate plan. Or worse yet, no consideration is even given to the ownership of property and the property seller or Title Company just sets it up this way for you when title is first taken.

With a smaller estate (we will see that size really does matter) this is often adequate basic estate planning. But, as time passes and the value of your assets march onward and upward, a husband and wife owning property in joint tenancy can have devastating tax disadvantages in trying to protect and preserve their assets.

DEATH & TAXES

Preserving your assets from the grips of huge IRS federal estate taxes is an important objective in protecting and preserving your assets.

The Internal Revenue Code allows spouses to transfer prop-

erty back and forth during their life or at death without tax consequences. And when one spouse dies all property can transfer
to the other spouse tax free, due to the unlimited marital deduction. However, the big estate tax burden arises when the second

You mean more
taxes again?

spouse dies, since there are taxes that must be paid by your
estate after it exceeds a certain dollar amount. This is referred
to as the unified tax credit.

In other words, estate values greater than a set dollar amount
are heavily taxed at an increasing rate. This is true even though
you paid income tax on the money when you first received it,
and then paid sales taxes on the assets when you purchased them.
And then, some day, good old Uncle Sam will want even more
taxes from you on this same money and property after you die,
figuring you won't be around to complain about it!

As we discussed in Chapter Two, the amount of taxes paid
on your savings and property are horrendous. We are at a point
in this country where 96% of the tax burden is shouldered by
50% of the people. The top 1% of income earners pay one third
of all income taxes, but they only earn 17% of the income. Add
to the unfair income tax burden the fact that the weight of death
taxes is grossly unfair since its acts as double taxation on the
same money and assets you already paid taxes on.

TAX RELIEF?

Two small pieces of good news on the horizon. First, as of

2006 you will be able to avoid estate taxation on amounts up to $1,000,000. Above this amount, the tax quickly jumps up to 55% of the amount over $1,000,000. While this amount might seem like a lot, keep in mind that in addition to savings and other investments, many people today are sitting with large amounts of equity in their first and second homes.

Add to the above amounts the proceeds of life insurance coverage often carried, and you see that it is no longer just the very wealthy that qualify to be added to the growing list to pay estate taxes for amounts greater than $1,000,000. Oftentimes, the amount of life insurance alone pushes even a smaller estate over the limit and creates a large estate tax burden.

So, including life insurance proceeds as part of your estate quickly increases the taxable amount and the estate tax burden to your family. Even with the increase in the dollar value to $1,000,000 which can be excluded from the taxation of your estate, inclusion of life insurance proceeds can quickly exceed the excluded amount.

In Chapter Thirteen you will see how you can keep life insurance from being taxed to your estate using Irrevocable Life Insurance Trusts. If, on the other hand, you have no objection to paying this multiple tax burden after you die, the rest of us continue to thank you for your generosity of adding to the pay-down of our national debt!

Thank you, thank you, and thank you.

But for those of us that desire to avoid estate taxes to the greatest extent legally possible, there is potentially some additional good news (albeit distant) being considered.

Congress continues to discuss eliminating the death tax burden, finally recognizing the inherent unfairness of this double taxation on families. During the 2000 election year this was a political hot potato with a majority of Congress, including Democrats, agreeing to such legislation. President Clinton, in his infinite wisdom, vetoed this bill.

We all need to keep a close eye on this activity with our new president and keep our legislators motivated to pass a similar bill. The good news is that at least the death tax is being discussed, as it affects more and more mainstream families and not just the extremely wealthy.

No Unemployed Estate Planners

Would estate planning be simplified, removing the need for lawyers and CPAs if the death tax was repealed? Hardly.

Estate planning and wealth preservation are not just about avoiding taxes. They're also about getting your assets to the right people in the right way. You will still need proper documentation such as Durable Powers of Attorney to assist you during times of a long term or short term disability. Living Wills would still be important to help keep you off of unnecessary or undesired life-support systems. And of course a Will and a Trust would still be required to designate who, how much, and when to distribute your wealth.

And most significantly, even if the estate tax is killed off, there are still reasons for using Trusts other than tax motivated purposes. For example, Trusts are great tools to protect assets from creditors, to provide for minor children, avoid probate, impose control on spendthrift heirs, and ensure that assets go to your children and not pass to the new wife or husband in a marriage after you die.

A final accounting of assets, their value, stepped up basis, capital gains, retirement and deferred plans will still need to be addressed and accounted for. Estate planning lawyers and CPAs will still have plenty of work to do.

WEALTH PRESERVATION TODAY

Until such time that the transfer tax is repealed, there is still wealth preservation planning you can do to protect and preserve your assets.

Today, the simplest and easiest method for married couples to protect and preserve their assets from estate tax burdens is by using Marital Bypass or A/B Trusts. This can be accomplished through either a Will or Living Trust, but remember that a Living Trust gives you more control of asset distribution by substantially reducing costs and increasing your privacy while avoiding probate.

MARITAL BY-PASS TRUST

Without going into all of the legal mumbo jumbo of how a Marital Bypass or A/B Trust works, understand that this is simply a plan where the first to die spouse retains their federally exempted amount allowing both spouses to retain their federal exemption. Without this planning, when the first spouses dies, the federal exemption is lost.

With proper planning, the result is that it doubles the federal exemption and excludes from taxation twice the amount otherwise realized. In essence, a married couple can double the amount of assets they pass to their children without incurring any estate tax burden at all if they properly plan ahead in advance.

With a Bypass or A/B Trust, the second surviving spouse is provided with income for life from the earlier created Trust and with power to appoint who will get the leftover principal. Subject to tax disincentives, the money in the Trust is always available to the surviving spouse. As you can imagine, these advanced estate planning techniques must be set up with great care, giving consideration to a multitude of planning issues.

Q-Tips

There exists another estate tax tool known as a qualified terminal interest trust, or a Q-TIP. With this type of Trust, your spouse's rights to property you leave behind comes to an end when he or she dies. If you follow the rules, this type of property transfer will qualify for the marital deduction even though the surviving spouse does not have full right of possession, enjoyment, and disposition in the property. In other words, your surviving spouse is given what is referred to as a life estate with this Trust asset.

Holographic Wills

I remember the brother of a deceased client that walked into my office one afternoon with a purported Will that was prepared in the hand of the deceased just before he died. All earlier Wills were claimed to be null and void and now everything went to the brother. Other family members were excluded. Was the Will legitimate? Did anyone care? You bet someone cared!

Wills written without the assistance of a lawyer can be a binding document in most states. This type of Will is called a Holographic Will. When certain fundamental requirements are met, they can and do pass title as set forth on the paper. However, too often the requirements of the Holographic Will are not properly met, or more often, they are disputed by other family members claiming that it is a sham or the deceased did not have requisite state of mind.

It turned out that the deceased's handwritten Will was in fact his last Will and Testament, even though it barely met the basic statutory requirements. The estate was not huge, but there was time and effort and costs incurred, defending against other heirs not included in this later Will.

While a handwritten Holographic Will is probably better than no Will at all, I would strongly encourage you to spend the time and money for proper legal advice on doing it right. And using a do-it-yourself guide to estate planning is not much better, since it rarely touches all bases needed for proper estate planning. Would you also do your own dental work or perform your own surgery?

FUNDING ESTATE PLANS

One of the biggest shortcomings of self-created estate plans is that retitling of assets is rarely completed and the Trust is most often not properly funded. These steps are essential to make certain that your estate plan is set up correctly. An unfunded, or improperly funded, estate plan is basically useless.

Spendthrift Provisions

This chapter would not be complete unless we at least covered the topic of a spendthrift provision. You can have an entire Will or Trust designed with this in mind, but at least this should be considered as part of your overall plan.

A spendthrift provision allows you to recognize that some people are not as good in managing money as others. Some would certainly waste assets away in a time far quicker than it took you to acquire them. Can you think of a few people who might be on this list? Here is your opportunity to exercise a certain degree of control, after your death, as to how the money should be distributed, if at all, and for what purposes.

The opportunities to exercise control after death are great, as long as the purposes are legal and not against public policy. For example, you would probably have a difficult time prohibiting your son or daughter from marrying someone based upon racial or religious grounds. But if the goals are not discriminatory or too difficult to put into place, then you can be very creative using spendthrift provisions.

Spendthrift provisions can easily go beyond designating restrictive distributions and instead set forth positive affirmative provisions. Many good estate planners, including myself, for years have set forth provisions that if a child graduates college or professional school by a certain age, then one-third distributions can be made, for example at ages 25, 30 and 35. However, if certain goals or objectives are not obtained by a certain age, then distributions are made at a much later date, for example ages 30, 40 and 45. This simple process can encourage a young adult to get a good education at a young age and learn good discipline before any money is handed over.

MOTIVATING YOUR HEIRS

Keeping heirs-apparent motivated with ambition and self-direction is becoming increasingly important, as the greatest wealth transfer in history is about to occur. Too often the talk behind closed doors during estate planning is the concern of creating a generation that lacks self reliance and confidence in themselves. You must remember that inheriting large sums of money arguably is destructive to your heir's self worth, even though their financial worth might be enhanced.

If you did not have the same ambition that you used to acquire the assets you have today, how different would your financial situation be?

By way of example I recall a young man, named Austin, who I have assisted with some of his financial affairs from time to time. Austin was the trust-fund recipient of approximately $10,000,000, and also stood to inherit approximately another $50,000,000 upon the death of his wealthy grandfather. This young man was in and out of drug and alcohol rehabilitation centers like revolving doors. When he was sober and off of drugs, which was not very often, he was a good man seeking to prove his own self worth, although not having the same ambition of a self-made individual.

More often than not, Austin was wasting his money and mind on wild pursuits, drugs and drinking. He had the opportunity to do great things from the wealth he inherited from his family fortune. Unfortunately, his father tried to manipulate him through strings in the Trust, where his inheritance was placed, and Austin fought all the harder against this authority. Today, I understand his father and he are doing better, but it is doubtful that he will ever have the drive and ambition that others create when they are forced to make ends meet on their own.

Some of the more advanced estate planning techniques include providing for a loan or partial distribution to a child for a home or business venture, if grounded with a sound business plan. This still provides an opportunity to assist the heir without losing sight of work ethics or long term planning. It helps them stay goal orientated. This might have been a useful technique for Austin instead of inheriting an enormous amount of money when he turned the legal age.

Setting Goals

Other advanced planning techniques include distribution of monies based upon achieving certain objectives. For example, annual distributions could be based upon annual income or gross volume of a new business venture. Distributions have also been tied to social or educational goals to encourage scholarly pursuits or social agendas. The goals and objectives can be left to your creativity.

Now I'm on target.

There are many other provisions that you can elect to include into a Will and Trust in an effort to have a properly established estate plan. Volumes can be written on this alone and are obviously beyond the scope of this book. But the key for you to remember is that if you have any interest or desire in protecting your money and property after your death, then a properly drafted and well-thought-out Will and Trust with the help of knowledgeable planners is essential.

Remember, you are not just planning the distribution of money, you are touching the lives of your loved ones after you are gone.

As you can see, the basics of a good estate plan consist of a properly drafted and organized Living Trust and a Will with pour or spill over provisions. The Trust should have all testamentary provisions set forth in the document. And to the extent that joint tenancy ownership is used to cause automatic transfers of property to avoid probate, great caution should be exercised to avoid tax traps and loss of control.

Beneficiary Designations

Make certain that proper beneficiary designations are made for life insurance, pensions, profit-sharing plans, IRAs and annuity survivor and death benefits and other pay-on-death proceeds. A proper beneficiary designation and when and how it should be utilized must be coordinated with your estate planners and decisions made consistent with your overall estate plan.

As discussed in the next chapter, a Durable Power of Attorney and a Medical Power of Attorney, accompanied by a Living Will are all essential to a basic estate plan.

IRA's

On the topic of IRA's and self-employed retirement plans, you should use great care in how they are integrated into your overall estate plan. Remember that distributions from an inherited IRA are subject to income taxes. The total tax on an inherited IRA can easily equal 70% or more when passing through an estate. Thus, a $100,000 IRA can be less that $30,000 when actually distributed to the heirs. Is it any wonder that the federal government promotes these estate planning tools?

Other Tools

Add-ons to your estate plan that you should consider are Anatomical Gifts, Letters of Instructions made to help organize your estate, a Testamentary Trust to manage your assets after your death, and Charitable Gifts and other gift planning to reduce estate taxes. The advantages of gifting is discussed in greater detail in Chapter Fourteen.

Importantly, remember to consider an appointment of a Guardian if there are minor children. Estates with a combined asset and insurance policy larger than $1,000,000 as of 2006 should consider the use of an Irrevocable Life Insurance Trust which is covered in Chapter Thirteen, and Family Limited Partnerships, corporations, and Limited Liability Companies for discounted gift giving.

THE "FOREVER TRUST"

Another trust finding its way around the estate planning and tax communities is known as the "Forever Trust". This Trust is designed to escape estate taxes as a result of new laws in several states by placing family wealth in a perpetual Trust. This Trust is supposed to protect wealth and allow it to accumulate for the benefit of family members forever.

In the past, it was not possible to create a Trust that would last forever because of the rule against perpetuities. That rule limits the maximum term of a Trust to 21 years measured by the end of a life in being. But now, as of the time of this writing, 11 states have repealed this rule and other states have similar legislation pending. To benefit from a perpetual Trust, you need not live in the state where the law was repealed; you can simply create the Trust in that state and have the Trust administered under the laws of that state.

A Forever Trust allows an enormous accumulation of wealth for future generations. For example, if you placed $1,000,000 into this Trust today and the rate of return was only 7%, in 100 years the Trust would have a value of $867,000,000. This allows a tremendous ability to help create and direct future generations, if this is one of your objectives.

The tax advantage of the Forever Trust is that future layers of estate taxes paid by each generation are completely eliminated. As wealth is passed on from one generation to the next estate taxes can wipe out 90% of all wealth in only three generations! Since wealth is placed into the Trust and not passed on generation to generation, estate taxes are completely eliminated.

However, two types of taxes in the Forever Trust must be planned around: estate taxes and generation skipping taxes. Since as of 2006 each person has a $1,000,000 estate tax exempt amount, this can be used to fund the trust, avoiding estate taxes. This amount can be doubled when a couple elects to each use their estate tax exempt amount when funding this Trust.

GENERATION SKIPPING

Generation skipping taxes (GST) is the other issue, since Congress passed a law years ago taxing estates an additional estate tax of up to 55%, when wealth transfers reach across multiple generations. But proper planning opportunities can avoid the GST burden, since every individual has a $1.03 million personal exemption from GST, which is indexed for inflation in future years. In other words, you can presently fund the Trust with up to $1.03 million with no GST.

A Forever Trust can become even more beneficial by funding it with life insurance and, with proper planning, these proceeds can escape being part of your taxable estate. More about the wonderful benefits of life insurance Trusts is found in Chapter Thirteen.

In using the Forever Trust, keep in mind that its terms are irrevocable, which means it cannot later be altered by you or beneficiaries if things change. However, you can give beneficiaries limited power over dispositions of the assets for succeeding generations. Also, you can provide a beneficiary the right to demand a 5% principal distribution annually. Both of these features add flexibility to the Trust for generations to come.

You will note that since a Trust must pay income taxes on the income it generates, planning strategies are generally geared towards appreciating assets. This type of portfolio fits well with holding family businesses or growth stock portfolio for later years. Appreciating assets are then only taxed one time when the assets are sold on a lower capital gains basis, instead of annually, as income is generated at a much higher level. As a result, growth in the Trust can be greater and faster.

Setting up a Forever Trust takes vision and planning. Using a qualified trustee that will appoint successive qualified trustees for the future takes resourcefulness and confidence. And since this Trust is a relatively new vehicle made possible only by the repeal of the rule against perpetuities, it must be carefully drafted with knowledgeable experts. But, as you can see by the opportunities to grow assets avoiding heavy estate taxes and GST, you have a tremendous opportunity to leave a legacy behind for future generations.

Trusts & More Trusts

Some of the more uncommon types of Trusts worthy of consideration are Minor's Trust for children, Dynasty Trusts, Grantor Retained Income Trusts (GRIT), Grantor Retained Annuity Trust (GRAT), Grantor Retained Unitrust (GRUT), and Qualified Subchapter S Trust (QSST) in uncommon situations for even more aggressive estate tax planning when trade-offs are acceptable and certain tax benefits can be achieved. Some of these are also noted in later chapters.

Significantly, each of the above tools can be fully integrated into offshore asset protection planning. You will learn in Section Three how this works when we focus on aggressive offshore planning to obtain aggressive asset protection.

Act Today

The choice of how, or if, you wish to see your assets preserved, is mostly left up to you. It is your choice. However, keep in mind, that if you fail to take the required steps to set forth your objectives, someone else will be making the choice of dividing up your money instead.

If you prefer to preserve what you have probably worked long and hard for over many years, you must stop today and take action now, before it is too late, otherwise you will have no say-so in the matter. Today, not tomorrow is the key.

What do you envision happening with all of your assets if you die tomorrow? Is what you desire able to occur? How would you change matters if you were to design the perfect plan for your family? Do you now realize that you can create a structure as you prefer? Are you prepared to act *now* if you really desire to reach these objectives?

And perhaps even more important, are you prepared at this very moment for a long or short term disability?

CHAPTER TWELVE

Disabilities & Your Assets

ALAN SHANEY WAS A ROBUST, HARD WORKING man. Before I moved my office and family to Vail, CO, Alan enthusiastically greeted me almost every morning in the lobby of our high rise office building in downtown Chicago. He was probably only two or three years older than me at the time, but he seemed to have the energy of a young stud bull set out to pasture with a bunch of beautiful cows.

Alan was a good-looking divorced man of about 40, healthy attitude, and carried himself well. Perhaps you know the type. Every morning when I saw Alan, he charged up and greeted me with a high energy and spirit.

Life is perfect

THE TRAGEDY

It was early one Monday morning when I received a telephone call from Alan's son, Jamie, just 20 years old and whom I had never met. He explained briefly to me on the telephone that something terrible had happened to his father over the weekend, that he had found my business card in his father's wallet, and could he immediately come into my office and talk with me.

When Jamie arrived at my office, he said that his father complained of a strong headache on Friday afternoon when he came home from work. So what else is new, I often had headaches on Friday afternoons. On Saturday it had grown more severe and he decided to visit the doctor's office. The doctor on-call immediately sent Alan to the emergency room and they scheduled him for surgery that same day for an aneurysm. No one had any idea of the lifestyle changes that Alan and his family were about to experience.

On Sunday morning when Alan awoke from surgery, he was unable to identify his own family members. He could barely utter basic words. The aneurysm was so severe that he could probably learn to walk again and regain some limited speech, but he would need constant care and attention. Even simple tasks like eating and bathing would be with the assistance of someone else. Now the family wanted to know what I could do to help with the legal issues.

Alan and I never spoke about estate planning or disability issues. And I learned that morning from Jamie that Alan had never spoken to any other attorney either about this important topic. There was not only no estate plan for Alan, but no plans had ever been made for any type of long or short term disability. Alan was still a very young, robust, and healthy middle aged-man with everything going for him, so why bother?

The only thing that could be legally done now was to open a disabled person's estate in the local Probate Court. All family assets and liabilities and sources of income and expenses were publicly accounted for, as they were now made a part of the public record for the world to see. Bonds had to be posted with the court, with annual renewal premiums. The court appointed another doctor for Alan to report his condition back to the judge.

It all took time and money, lots of time and money, before the judge agreed to issue an order of court appointing a guardian for Alan.

Until a guardian was appointed for Alan, health care decisions and financial matters had to be placed on hold. Since Alan had lost his capacity to act, someone needed to be appointed with full power and legal capacity to act for Alan and make decisions for him. Once the court finally issued an order appointing Alan's son Jamie as his guardian, then health care discussions and financial issues could finally be addressed.

Even after the court initially appointed the guardian for the initial decisions, the guardian was required to file updated financial and health care decisions on a regular basis with the court. This is part of the accountability that a fiduciary has to the court for these types of appointments. This took more time and money, and continued to expose all financial information and health issues to the public. The family felt this was not fair, but nothing else could be done.

DURABLE POWER OF ATTORNEYS

What Alan should have done, and what you should immediately do if you have not yet done so, is to have in place a properly executed Durable Power of Attorney. This document is significantly more powerful than a typical general power of attorney.

By contrast, the general power of attorney is only good for the agent as long as the principal is alive, has not revoked the power to act, or has the mental capacity to continue as a principal. When any situation arises that reduces or eliminates the capacity of a principal, the power granted to the agent is generally destroyed and the agent can no longer act on the principal's behalf under a general power of attorney.

But the Durable Power of Attorney is a very special power that is granted to an agent. Its purpose is specifically designed to come into effect when the principal's capacity no longer exists. Until and unless incapacity occurs in the principal, the agent has no power to act.

Had Alan signed a Durable Power of Attorney, a family member could have presented it to the doctors and representatives at the hospital and moved forward immediately with making decisions. Mortgages and other financial obligations would not have gone unpaid for months until the court issued its order appointing the guardian. The time and the costs, and the legal fees of proceeding in court for the appointment of a guardian, could all have been avoided. The legal fees were now in the thousands of dollars.

And of course, the emotional trauma that the family went through could have been lessened by not having to deal with the ongoing court issues.

It is important that you select a person that you have a great amount of trust for as your agent under the Durable Power of Attorney. The person you select could be making life or death decisions for you. You need to discuss these issues with them today, just in case.

And too, the Durable Power of Attorney can and should provide authority to your agent, to act on your behalf to write checks, so that financial obligations are not neglected. You will need to not only have trust and respect for this person, but they should also be aware of your private affairs. Simple, yet important matters such as locating financial documents and funds should be discussed.

HEALTHY REASONS

In the mountain ski community where I live is a wonderful man, named Peru, who during the 1970's won a number of gold medals representing his country skiing in the Olympics. To this day, he is extremely active, both athletically and mentally. He is as strong physically, as he is headstrong. This I personally will attest to, since as a friend and client we have argued over minor points in healthy debates.

This great Olympic Champion, now in his 50's, suffered a mild stroke one day, and now has great difficulty in walking and talking and even remembering names of close friends. Fortunately, Peru had the foresight to have a properly executed Durable Power of Attorney in place, and his family is able to assist with his financial and medical needs while he is trying to recover. Are you prepared for one of life's surprises?

Remember that the Durable Power of Attorney does not come into play until and unless a short or long term disability occurs. There is plenty of protection for you until a disability sets in, as long as it is properly drafted, since it requires two doctors to certify your incapacity. But since you never know if and when a disability could occur, it is essential that you take the necessary steps *now* before it is to late if you are interested in protecting and preserving your assets, and perhaps more importantly, your life.

SHORT TERM DISABILITIES

Everyone does not suffer a long term disability. More common would be a short term disability, which can be just as catastrophic. The same health care and financial issues are prevalent.

The insurance industry claims that those of us in the middle age category have a ten times greater likelihood of suffering a disability than dying during this time of our life. Ten times greater!

If you think about how much money you might make in your lifetime, you'll realize that your ability to earn is surely one of your most important assets. What would it cost you if you suddenly became unable to work? If you haven't properly protected yourself against disability, you're placing your financial security at risk.

Living Wills

Along these same lines is another document that you should have in place today to help protect and preserve your assets called a Living Will. This document name is really a misnomer. A Living Will serves the purpose of avoiding keeping someone alive artificially, when death is all but imminent. For some, there are religious issues attached to the direction, but for most this is not a problem.

It is a fact of life that hospitals are operated like businesses with a bottom line profit incentive. They and the doctors that work hard to serve you are greatly concerned with being sued. Decisions are made daily that reflect their concerns for profit and liability.

Do you believe for one moment that the doctor or the hospital representative is willing to make the decision to take you off of an artificial life support system when your wishes are unknown or uncertain? Think again!

If you wish to avoid being placed on a artificial life support system when death is imminent, you must make this declaration clear today in a document known as a Living Will. This form simply informs the doctors and the hospital representatives to "pull the plug" if death is all but certain. The amount of emotional trauma and financial burden that this little form can preclude is beyond description.

PAINFUL CONSEQUENCES

Just ask Mrs. Harkney, as she flew in from a small town in Ohio and waited for her son John, age 25, to slowly die with some dignity in a large Chicago hospital. Day after day she would call me by telephone from John's bedside and ask me what we could legally do to avoid the pain and suffering, as John lay in bed with an irreversible disease taking its final toll. She spent weeks of heart-wrenching agony watching her son slowly die, as he was being kept "alive" by some damn mechanical device.

The legal option of going through the time and expense to get a court order to cut off the artificial life support system was too emotional a step for her to take. Instead, she watched and watched and cried and cried. Eventually, even the artificial system could do no more and peace was there at last for John. But for Mrs. Harkney, it took much too long and too great a toll, both emotionally and financially.

A Living Will signed by John when he was healthy could have reduced or prevented the misery that his mother experienced. His direction to limit artificial life support, if properly made early on, could have preserved his estate and the finances of his mother, perhaps hundreds of thousands of dollars and the untold amount of pain and suffering she went through during the final chapter of John's life.

Plan Ahead

Alan and John failed to have any stateside planning to help protect their assets, or themselves, in the event of a disability. However Peru, having lived part of his life abroad, thought in a more worldly fashion. Offshore planning did not seem so mysterious and foreign to him.

Peru had in place a combination of stateside and offshore planning to help protect and preserve his assets. Not only did he have a stateside Durable Power of Attorney in place, but it was integrated as part of an overall offshore asset protection plan that would allow him or his family to quickly move assets offshore in the event of a major financial catastrophe. The world of offshore Trusts is explored in Section Three.

Have you prepared your Durable Power of Attorney and Living Will to avoid emotional and financial hardships? Is it current and up-to-date? Do you understand the importance of tending to these issues *now* and not later? What are you waiting for? What is your family waiting for?

Generally, life insurance is taken out for purposes of providing for a spouse or children when you die. This can be a costly mistake if not properly structured. Now, let's explore how you can avoid having life insurance proceeds eat up the value of your estate.

CHAPTER THIRTEEN

Life Insurance Eroding Your Wealth

IF PROLONGED DEATH AND AGONY ARE NOT ENOUGH, let's add to it the weight of placing even greater amounts of estate taxes upon life insurance proceeds, a planning tool designed to lessen burdens after you die. Life insurance is often acquired to make sure the kids get through college, the mortgage is eliminated, a burial is paid for, or for many other important needs.

LIFE INSURANCE & TAX BURDENS

Did you know that by taking out life insurance you can be significantly *increasing* the estate tax burden on your family?

Life insurance can be taxed in your estate up to a whopping

215

55%! Why? As stated earlier in this book, estate taxes are as high as 55%. While life insurance is not taxable to the recipients directly, it becomes an estate tax burden by virtue of the statutory requirement to include life insurance proceeds in your gross estate. IRS Estate Tax Form 706 is one of the last tax forms that will be filed on your behalf after you die.

If you plan for money to be available to pay your estate taxes, reduce mortgages, or get the kids through college, you may fall far short of that goal if you are generating estate taxes equal to more than one-half of life insurance proceeds. That's right, over one-half, 55% of your life insurance proceeds can become the amount of additional estate tax burden you create for your family upon your death.

When you consider that the amount of equity in our homes, the savings and investments owned, all other assets held, and add to this the amount of your life insurance policy proceeds, they can quickly add up to a taxable estate. As of 2006 this amount is $1,000,000. Above that amount, without proper estate planning, the estate taxes quickly run up to 55% of the total.

Most life insurance agents fail to tell you this side of the story when they sell you a policy. But good insurance agents are estate wise and will advise you accordingly.

Eliminating Insurance Tax Burdens

Before you pick up the telephone and call your insurance agent and give him or her your piece of mind, you should know that there are certain things that you can do to completely eliminate the estate tax burden associated with life insurance, and accomplish the goals you set out to do with the proceeds.

An Irrevocable Life Insurance Trust (commonly called an ILIT) is a Trust used to own life insurance policies. You then make annual gifts into the Trust, and the Trust in turn can pay the annual premiums for the policy. Once the ILIT is set up, it cannot be materially changed or terminated without some complicated steps. If properly designed, upon your death, the life insurance proceeds will be paid to the Trust and disbursed according to the Trust provisions.

In this chapter we will look at stateside planning using ILITs. In Chapter Twenty Two we will see how this same concept can be expanded upon for offshore planning for asset protection and wealth preservation. The stateside techniques discussed here will help provide you with the fundamental principles before we proceed with strictly offshore planning. Keep in mind that the fully integrated estate plan uses both stateside and offshore asset protection planning tools.

Irrevocable Life Insurance Trusts

There are some tricky legal issues to work around with an ILIT, so good competent legal advice is essential. It is important that you do not retain what is called indicia of ownership of the life insurance policy, and instead that it is the Trust that owns the policy. You cannot be the trustee of the ILIT.

After you make annual gift giving to the Trust for purposes of making payments for the premiums, the named beneficiaries must be given notice that money has been added to the Trust and that they have a set number of days to withdraw the money if they choose. This notice is usually referred to as a "Crummy Letter" named after a precedent setting case before the Supreme Court.

Another alternative is a second-to-die insurance policy which covers both spouses, but pays nothing until the second spouse dies. The payout can then be used to pay off taxes, college education, mortgages or other purposes. The combined amount of the estate for the spouses must be large enough to justify this type of policy.

Most importantly, the ILIT will avoid probate and not be part of your taxable estate. The ILIT is also an excellent tool to provide liquidity to your estate. The objectives you initially set out to accomplish, for example a mortgage pay-off, college education, burial provisions, etcetera, can all be accomplished without increasing estate tax burdens.

If you desire to keep your estate taxes minimized, preserving your assets after you die, then an Irrevocable Life Insurance Trust is another tool that should be used in your estate planning. Remember that there are costs associated with setting up and administering the Trust, but these are generally small by comparison to the amount of the estate taxes you can save.

And Yes, More Trusts

Mentioned earlier in Chapter Eleven were some other types of Trusts to help reduce your estate tax burdens. They were the GRIT, GRAT, GRUT, and QSST, all are important vehicles to preserve assets. Understand that Trusts have been around for a long time and are not a new concept. Some promoters simply re-label a Trust that has been around for years and sell it under a new name.

Some types of Trusts arise because of a change in the tax code or because a new idea or concept comes into play and opportunities are taken advantage of before the IRS closes off what are perceived as unfair practices. The bottom line is that before you go through the effort and cost of establishing a Trust, make certain that you are comfortable with what is being provided, how the objectives will be accomplished, and how it will work for you.

The Crat

Worthy of note, one of the so-called tried and proven Trusts, called a Charitable Remainder Annuity Trust (referred to as a CRAT), includes a remainder interest to charities in exchange for a current tax deduction and an income stream during your life. The amount of the deduction depends upon your life expectancy and interest rates used. The income will depend upon your age, whether the annuity covers one life or two, and the amount of the gift.

THE CRT

And too, a Charitable Remainder Trust (referred to as a CRT) is designed to pay a set dollar amount, either for life or up to 20 years. When the beneficiaries die, the balance left in the Trust goes to charity. If the trustee sells the appreciated property placed in the Trust, you can benefit from an increase in income paid to you as well. The size of the charitable deduction you take when you set up the Trust is figured using government valuation rules.

The obvious benefit is that you can use some of these vehicles to place significantly appreciated assets, like stocks, into it and potentially reap large financial gain without paying capital gains on the appreciation.

THE CLT

With a Charitable Lead Trust (referred to as a CLT), a charity of your choosing gets annual income for a specified number of years. When the Trust ends, then the beneficiaries get what is left over. The advantage is that the gift to your heirs is valued at a reduced gift tax cost, based upon IRS tables, since your heirs do not benefit until some time in the future.

The rules and requirements on any of these types of Trust are strict and complex. And, since there is often great opportunity to protect and preserve large amounts of wealth in these Trusts, you can count on the fact that the IRS scrutinizes them closely. Therefore, you must make certain that they are set up and administered correctly.

Think Synergy

But as you can see, setting up the right type of Trust and combining it with charitable purposes can greatly enhance your program to protect and preserve your assets. And using some of the above stateside Trusts, particularly the ILIT, can provide even greater benefits when going offshore as you will see in Chapter Twenty Two.

Did you know that outright gifting of your money and property can also help protect and preserve your assets? The next chapter helps identify some of these gifting tools to further help you protect and preserve your wealth.

CHAPTER FOURTEEN

Giving to Preserve

OW DOES "GIVING" YOUR MONEY AWAY PRESERVE your assets? Good question. Let us look at several tools in advanced onshore stateside estate planning that can help preserve your estate by *gifting* assets away. Of course these tools can be integrated into offshore asset protection planning as well.

GIFTING TO CHILDREN

If you have a goal to pass as much of your assets to your children as possible, and still have plenty of money to enjoy a comfortable retirement for yourself, then gifting may be an option for you. There are several methods of gifting that might work to preserve and protect a portion of your estate.

Remember that if the key is to preserve your estate for the next generation, then making gifts to them can help get the job done.

THE GIFTING FORMULA

First, the easy formula. Each of us has a right to gift $10,000 per year, indexed for inflation as of 1999, to each recipient without gift tax consequences to us. Of course, there are no income tax consequences to any recipient of our gifts, no matter how much we give them. With spousal contributions, a husband and wife can gift $20,000 per year to each child, year after year.

While the gift is not tax deductible, you pay no taxes when the gift is made. Not only is the gifted amount removed from your estate, but the income it generates will be taxed to the recipient. If gifts are made to children, the income is taxed at their lower tax rate. Gifts for amounts over the annual limits may be taxable to you and you will need to file an IRS Form 709 Gift Tax Return.

Part of the beauty of gifting to your heirs, is that over time, $20,000, year after year with income or dividend growth, can have sizable benefits of wealth preservation. Over just five years alone you can gift $100,000 to a child, and the growth in that principal amount can be tremendous.

A lifetime of gifting, say over twenty or thirty years, with accumulated earnings and considering tax savings, could yield amounts of $500,000 to $1,000,000, or more. And most importantly, this amount will not be included in your estate when you die. As you can see, the potential for preservation of assets, especially with growth, with regular gifting, is substantial.

More Gifts?

If some is good is not more better? Oftentimes with regards to estate tax savings, the answer is yes. There is an even larger amount that you can gift away, combined with the potential for growth and tax savings in the child's name, that is potentially greater than with the small gift-giving formula explained above.

In addition to annual gifting amounts described above, each of us is allowed what is referred to as a unified gift and estate tax credit. This is a one time credit against the value of your assets you can take either during your life or upon your death. This credit, in essence, reduces your estate tax burden. In 1997 it was $192,800 and by 2006 Congress agreed to adjust it to $321,300. As of 2006, this equates to the first $1,000,000 of your estate not becoming taxable upon your death.

Any amount of your estate excluded from estate taxes leaves greater amounts of assets for your heirs. Remember dollars you gift to your heirs are tax free. And by using your unified gift and estate tax credit, you preserve your estate even more by not having this amount subject to estate taxes. So the good news is that your estate might not owe any taxes for the equivalent amount of $1,000,000, plus amounts gifted per couple per receipt for each year in the amount of $20,000, if you use proper planning.

In other words, there is a tremendous opportunity of adding to the annual gift giving by making sizable gifts to your heirs, using up your unified gift and estate tax credit. Keep in mind that the growth of the gifts to your heirs will be in their name and taxable at their often lower tax rate and not yours. As the size of the gift grows over the years due to the income it generates, it will be in their name and taxable to them.

CONTROLLING THE GIFTS

If you are naturally concerned about handing over large sums of money to your underage children, worry not. You need not make direct gifts to your children in an effort to preserve the value of your estate. You can establish a custodial account using either the Uniform Gift to Minors Act (UGMA) or the Uniform Transfer to Minors Act (UTMA). If properly established, the UGMA or the UTMA will protect the accumulation of the assets while they are minors.

There are generally no charges to set up or administer either the UGMA or UTMA. You can add to them and build it up regularly, as you see fit, without owing gift taxes, as long as you add no more than the annual exempt amount. Year after year, these vehicles can be used to help preserve the amount of assets that you pass to your children and reduce your estate taxes, ultimately preserving more and more of your assets.

Another great advantage to setting up UGMA or UTMA accounts for your heirs is that you can add assets that are not income producing. For example, you can add real estate or paintings, in addition to stocks, bonds, or mutual funds. The growth in value of these assets will be available to your children in the future.

Remember that you must live with the fact that your minor children will take control of these assets when they reach legal age. The legal age is 18 or 21, depending on the state you live in. But, you are not legally required to liquidate the accounts and hand them over to your children just because they reach legal age. However, if they demand the right to these assets, it is their legal right.

And remember too, that any assets that your children have in their names can potentially reduce their eligibility for college aid. Further, if you die before the child reaches maturity, the value of the accounts will still be taxed under your estate, completely defeating your intentions unless you name another adult, to act as the custodian. Also, since children under the age of 14 are taxed at their parents tax level, you should consider giving growth assets instead of incoming producing assets.

Wealth Preservation & Gifts

So how does gifting your assets away protect and preserve your wealth? Simple.

Since the assets you gift away are no longer in your name, they are not subject to attack by creditors should litigation arise. This type of asset protection planning is often started in small amounts and can grow in value over the years. You can transfer assets into your children's name in the form of annual gift giving, or convey into stateside or offshore vehicles designed with the same intended purpose in mind. In either event, the result of protecting and preserving your assets in the event of a financial catastrophe can be accomplished.

Beyond the above gift giving ideas to preserve your assets for future generations and for asset protection planning purposes, you should also consider some special categories of gift giving.

For example, if you or an elderly grandparent wish to make a gift to pay for the college education of your child, this is possible. The tax exempt gift must be made directly to the college or university equal to the cost of the tuition. The understanding is that the student's tuition is considered paid. However, the gift must be for tuition only, and cannot be used for room and board. Since tuition is generally the largest expense while attending college, this is a great opportunity for gifting.

The same option also exists for the paying of someone else's hospital bill. The process is simply known as a qualified transfer, and as of this writing there do not appear to be any catches, at least not yet. Plus these amounts do not limit your right to give up to the exempt amount per year, to the beneficiary of the transfer, as a tax exempt gift.

GIFTING & FAMILY LIMITED PARTNERSHIPS

Another important approach to using gifts to pass valuable property to your children and for asset protection planning is to create a Family Limited Partnership. Remember Family Limited

Partnerships we discussed in earlier chapters? Remember synergy? Always think about how tools and techniques can be integrated in such a way to take advantage of their synergy.

And synergy?

As we discussed in Chapter Ten, the use of a Family Limited Partnership allows you to retain complete control of the family business or the partnership asset. You then have a number of options as to what you do with the limited partnership interests. The limited partners have no control or say-so over the management of the assets.

Each year, each of the General Partners, you and your spouse, can gift away partnership interests, reducing your share of the assets. And, the General Partners are allowed to gift these shares at an often sizable discount to face value, since the shares are generally not readily marketable to the public.

For example, a cash gift could be closer to $14,000 or $15,000, instead of the $10,000 limit (before being annually adjusted for inflation). The discount is legitimate if there's a valid business purpose for the partnership and you can justify the size of the discount. Importantly, if the recipients are minority holders of the partnership, which is generally the case, then minority discounts could even make the true value of the gift to them even greater.

Like the above gifting with the annual $10,000 limits and the unified gift and estate tax credits, over a period of years the gifting of limited partnership interests can be sizable. And too, the value increases year after year in the name of the recipient and not your name, so that this continues to reduce the size of your taxable estate and ultimately the estate tax burden.

SEEDS OF GROWTH

What better way to protect and preserve your money and property than to gift it away early on, year after year, let it grow in the name of your children, and then you continue to control the underlying assets? Remember, these are your assets, and what you do with them is your choice. But, the earlier you start, the more you are able to accomplish your goals. Why wait?

And remember, you can accomplish the above objectives without leaving your hometown, or without any offshore planning. All gifting can be completed locally, using stateside planners and institutions. Of course if you prefer the advantages using enhanced offshore asset protection planning discussed in Section Three, then this can be achieved as well, providing you even greater benefits, as discussed, using offshore asset protection planning techniques.

Hopefully by now you recognize that there are many different types of techniques and tools available to the average person in trying to protect and preserve hard earned money. The average person of means is self-made and often seeks to be in charge of their destiny. Some of the tools are right for you, and others are not. It depends on your particular facts and circumstances. It also depends on your objectives and how serious you are in protecting your assets.

SETTING GOALS & ACTING NOW

But the key to any of the asset protection tools that we have discussed so far is that you can not sit idly by. Reading and learning and understanding the concepts is only a small, first step. The biggest and most important step is to take charge in protecting and preserving your wealth, whatever level it is, and not lose it to some flim-flam catastrophe. You must act now and take every reasonable measure you can to preserve it for yourself in later years, or for the next generation. Taking action *today* is the next critical step.

Taking action today may mean for you to start with stateside planning and then growing into offshore asset protection techniques. Or, it may mean that you want to immediately proceed with the best asset protection planning tools available and go directly to offshore planning using many of the tools we have discussed so far. Wherever your level of comfort lies, you must still take the first step and take necessary action to implement your objectives.

LEARNING & UNDERSTANDING

Hopefully your first step in implementing asset protection planning is trying to understand what options are available to you. Perhaps reading this book is your next step. But do not end your journey here. Move on to the next step and begin with interviewing professionals that specialize in the area of asset protection planning and work daily with the tools and techniques discussed in this book.

231

Section One of the book mainly dealt with applying various state and federal laws to your benefit for asset protection planning in a stateside fashion. This means that these issues generally arise by virtue of living or doing business in the US and what steps you can take to apply these laws to protect and preserve your assets.

Section Two of this book looked at asset protection planning in another way. This section considered how you can prevent natural events in life from wiping out your assets. Importantly, these steps can be implemented using stateside asset protection planning, or can be integrated into more aggressive offshore planning which will be explored in more detail in Section Three.

As you next read through Section Three on offshore planning, think how you can accomplish your objectives of asset protection planning by integrating the tools discussed so far into offshore planning.

Remember that death is a natural part of living. Think about how properly drafted Wills and Trusts can be used in your situation to help create privacy and protection for you and your family. Think about how you can legitimately use these tools to avoid estate taxes and build asset protection fortresses around your assets. How could retitling of your assets, while retaining a high degree of control over them, possibly save them from creditors or allow your estate to save large fees and expenses in the event of a major lawsuit or death? How can you accomplish some of the goals today you seek for your loved ones after you die?

Assuming that you have many good years ahead of you,

how might you protect your assets while you are alive if you suffered a long or short term disability today? Think creatively how you might benefit by having your assets held in the name of an offshore Trust, your Trust, if this disability was creating a financial burden on you or your family threatening to thrust you into a financial cesspool.

Remember Irrevocable Life Insurance Trusts. While successfully used for many years stateside to avoid increasing taxes burdens on your estate, think how you might expand this concept by going offshore for enhanced asset protection planning.

GOING OFFSHORE

Finally, if you are considering gifting your assets to your heirs or for asset protection planning, why not expand that planning by considering to go offshore. If asset protection planning is good for you, is it not important for your heirs as well?

Why do Americans think so narrowly when it comes to our asset preservation? Europeans and Asians in particular, invest a significant portion of their money outside of their boundaries, inside and outside of the US, as a normal way of doing business. Why then, do Americans naively believe that safety stops at our shores?

Most Americans do not invest or utilize asset protection planning beyond their backyard because they mistakenly believe that the best is right here at home. In reality, the American legal and tax system is remarkably abusive to successful individuals who have worked hard to achieve what they have accomplished. Looking beyond the boundaries of the US can and does provide opportunities for asset preservation that you will never find at home.

In the next, or third section of this book on asset protection planning and wealth preservation, we will look at some of the most advanced asset protection techniques available today. Going offshore should not be foreign to you.

You will learn how the concept of synergy can really come into play if you are serious in your pursuits to protect and preserve your assets. Open your mind and use your imagination in how you can integrate the concepts in Sections One and Two into offshore asset protection to aggressively protect your assets.

Discover the world you have been missing by looking for asset protection planning offshore.

SECTION THREE

ADVANCED ASSET PROTECTION PLANNING

(GOING OFFSHORE)

CHAPTER FIFTEEN

Who Needs Offshore Planning?

R EMEMBER WHY YOU DECIDED TO INVEST YOUR time to read this guide about protecting and preserving assets? If you have made it this far, I would bet on the fact that you are serious minded in protecting your assets.

I will also bet that you either have a high level of net worth or a high income level, or both. If not, you are probably on your way to these goals and are thinking ahead.

Perhaps you are concerned that you are in a higher risk business or profession, or you are now looking towards retirement with some peace of mind. In any event, you probably seek to aggressively protect and preserve your assets from the jaws of the sharks. These are all reasons to seek aggressive asset protection planning.

What are the potential problems that you are faced with that drive the need for aggressive asset protection planning? Why look offshore? Why do you need to plan ahead at all? Why do you need a Plan B when you have a good master plan afloat?

LITIGATION GONE CRAZY

First, remember that litigation in America is a popular pastime. The legal system in many respects has run amuck. The number of lawsuits in America are growing at a pace seven times greater than the population. Ex-employee claims against prior employers are multiplying like rabbits. And large medical malpractice awards are exceeding professional liability coverage in 40% of the claims.

With the population in America at approximately 250,000,000 men, women and children, at any given time there are 100,000,000 active lawsuits nationwide. 30,000,000 new lawsuits are filed each year. Most lawsuits take between 24 months to 48 months to resolve, and in particular, tort cases can take up to 5 years.

And the creativity with plaintiff's legal counsel and the willingness of juries and judges to find liability against defendants like you and me continues unabated. Have we all gone mad?

Without picking on the medical profession, but by way of example, 13% of all surgeons are sued every year, with obstetricians and gynecologists sued at a rate of 16% each and every year. As a group, 65% of all gynecologists are sued during their professional career. A popular cause of action against these groups is for emotional distress, and awards for severe emotional deficiency verdicts exceed $1,000,000 in 80% of the verdicts!

Physicians are certainly not alone. One of the latest popular rages arise from claims from ex-employees against former employers, increasing by 20% annually, and they are winning big time. This year alone, ex-employees will sue 3 out of 5 companies, a solid 60%. Business owners and managers will need to endure on average over 3 years of depositions, discovery, trial preparation and much, much more during the litigation process.

The costs are high even if the case is settled, and the awards by this latest ex-employee litigation fad can be devastating.

Recall the employee litigation case discussed in an earlier chapter made by a Florida female telephone sex operator that was awarded $30,000.00 when she developed a repetitive motion injury due to masturbating herself daily while speaking to clients on the telephone? Can litigation get any wackier? What protection do you believe you have against weird lawsuits from your employees?

RISK LOSING IT ALL

And the US is the land of the free? The sad truth is that freedom and privacy is merely a dream. The reality is that you

241

are foolish if you do not take aggressive steps to protect and preserve your hard-earned assets.

Just one lawsuit could wipe you or your business out financially. Years of hard work with plans for retirement or wealth preservation for future family generations can go up in smoke overnight. The larger the target you become financially, the easier it becomes for others to justify filing a suit against you. Your chances of being sued over the next several years are very high.

These are not just concerns for the ultra-rich, but for anyone that owns a business, runs their own profession, is a high-income wage earner, or who has accumulated some level of wealth.

SEEKING ALTERNATIVES

Some of the objectives that you can accomplish with an aggressive offshore asset protection plan include reaching a higher level of financial privacy regarding holdings and future investment. You can minimize the financial impact of a lawsuit. You can minimize or avoid altogether problems with friends, business associates, spouses or lovers, or similar claimants.

Further, you can avoid unforeseen changes in the political climate of the United States. You can avoid the potential imposition of exchange controls or other limitations on the free movement of assets beyond stateside borders. And there are certainly opportunities for tax savings from the implementation of certain investment strategies, although the principal purpose of asset protection planning is not tax motivated.

Your Choice

Remember we started at the beginning of this book with the concept that what you do with your assets is your business as long so you are doing it legally and not defrauding others. Protecting and preserving your assets is your legal right, and you need not feel like you are doing something wrong when you take aggressive steps.

By doing nothing you will be exposing your assets, but by taking action today, well in advance of problems that can and do occur, you can protect and preserve your assets as you see fit.

Your Legal Right to Protect Assets

An underlying legal principle in American law is that until a creditor has established title, he has no right to control a debtor's assets. Since the 18th century, American courts have consistently refused to grant general creditors a preliminary injunction to restrain a debtor's asset transfers that allegedly would defeat satisfaction of any anticipated judgment.

The US Supreme Court relied upon the above long established legal principle in Grupo Mexicano (decided in July 1999), and refused to allow a preliminary injunction in favor of a creditor against a debtor. The court reiterated that since 1789, first established in the Federal Judiciary Act of 1789, that preliminary injunctive relief was beyond the equitable jurisdiction of the courts, and that a creditor has no interest in a debtor's property without first obtaining a judgment. Further, the court stated, that a debtor could do what he wanted with his property until such time as a judgment was obtained against him.

As recent as March 2000, in <u>Credit Agricole Indosuez v. Rossiyskiy Kredit Bank,</u> debtors attempted to remove their assets from the US jurisdiction prior to a judgment where three European Banks were trying to collect on a $30,000,000 Russian promissory note. The New York's highest court refused to consider the plaintiff's argument that the assets would be difficult to locate after any judgment could be attained. This court held that New York Court cannot be used to freeze global assets of a debtor prior to a judgment.

And too, in Florida, the Supreme Court in <u>Bayview Estates Corporation</u> (a 1934 case) established that *"the mere fact that a person may be indebted to another does not render a conveyance of his property a fraud in law upon his creditors. The owner of property, whether real or personal, possesses the absolute right to dispose of all or any part of it as he sees fit."*

What the above decisions make clear, is that you have an absolute legal right to transfer your property, as long as that property is freely alienable. Undoubtedly, the decisions in Grupo Mexicano, Credit Agricole Indosuez, and Bayview Estates Corporation support asset protection planning at both a state and federal level in the United States. Asset protection planning is not only your legal right, it is a great American tradition.

Think Synergy

You have already seen some examples of how synergy, the act of combining effective tools and techniques together, can and do help protect and preserve assets. There is not just one way for an artist to apply the basic colors on a canvas to create a masterpiece. There is not one method of organizing musical notes to create a classical composition.

Synergy is taking the place over already.

And too, there is not a unified method of organizing or using legal planning tools and techniques together, to accomplish a successful asset protection and preservation plan. Any planner that tells you that he or she has the perfect plan, the tried and true formula, should be approached cautiously. Better yet, probably avoided.

You have already witnessed how taxes, litigation, personal guarantees, and how you conduct your personal and business relationships can and do make a big impact on your asset preservation. Remember the importance of how you own property with someone else, the special issues of the assets of the elderly, and the benefits of multiple business structures all come into play in wealth preservation.

Remember, not if, but when the calamity strikes, how you have implemented a plan, and where you elect to live, and how

245

you attempt to resolve financial issues, all greatly determine how you weather the storm.

Issues of death and dying are all part of protecting and preserving your wealth. Common tools of life insurance can add to the already burdensome formula of estate taxes unless set aside in a separate Trust. And gifting, while at first blush appears to be counterproductive in preserving your assets, is a potentially great tool to actually protect and preserve assets for future generations and to avoid estate tax burdens.

And importantly, the synergy of properly combining legal techniques and acting now, makes all the difference, if you truly desire to protect and preserve your money and property.

TRUTH ABOUT STATESIDE PLANNING

Notwithstanding all of the positive opportunities to protect and preserve your assets that have already been discussed, the real truth is that owning and controlling your assets by these vehicles stateside, without going offshore, has certain limitations. While each and every one, or a combination thereof, can help you achieve some level of asset protection preservation, none can offer you the asset protection that you can achieve by going beyond the four-corners of the US boundaries.

In other words, stateside planning is important, but only as a first step.

LIMITS ON STATESIDE PLANNING

For example, a Living Trust, while providing great opportunity to assist with wealth preservation by keeping your estate out of probate and allowing someone else to care for you or a loved one, is not an asset protection vehicle per se. And even the Spendthrift Trust discussed has limitations, since some states ignore it altogether. In those states where it is recognized, once the money has been distributed to the beneficiary, it is open game to claimants.

And too, the Family Limited Partnership, while a tremendous asset protection planning vehicle to help discourage creditors, and also providing wonderful opportunities for estate planning, in some situations has proven useless where a judge has disregarded the structure. Corporations too, if legal formalities are not strictly followed can be pierced, allowing plaintiffs to get directly to you, the owner. Liability and umbrella insurance often times do not cover the type of claim made. Also, you often can find yourself underinsured.

Gifting away your assets is limited to only those assets you legally transfer to others not in violation of fraudulent transfer laws, and can also leave you with insufficient retirements funds. Your spouse or friends today, having knowledge of your Plan B which is designed to preserve your assets, can become your worst enemy tomorrow by sharing your information with the rest of the world.

Homestead and bankruptcy exemptions obviously cannot preserve all of your assets; they can only assist with preserving those within the state and federal guidelines that are preplanned and qualified.

Stateside asset protection laws, initially started in Alaska,

Nevada and Delaware, simply do not place your assets outside of the reach of US Courts, leaving your assets within US boundaries for plaintiff hungry lawyers. Even the best team of lawyers that you think you can count on for your defense, might not be able to protect you when you need them the most.

The bottom line is that if you limit your asset protection planning to stateside planning, then you are placing grave limitations on your asset protection planning. Without a doubt all of the techniques explored earlier are good starting points in a plan to protect and preserve your assets, but just like running a marathon race, the starting line and the finish line are a long way apart.

GOING OFFSHORE

So what should you do? If you are serious about protecting and preserving your assets, it is essential that you take the next logical step and look at the many opportunities offered offshore. International investing and wealth preservation should not be foreign to you. If you have not already started to integrate asset protection planning techniques from around the world, you should start considering this today.

Going international! If you are not well traveled, you might start slowly, one step at a time. For the more experienced travelers, your concept of the different cultures and how things are done is perhaps more refined. In any event, open your eyes to the world of opportunities that surround you for more aggressive asset protection planning.

What are the more advanced techniques that are commonly used today by the very wealthy to protect and preserve their assets? Where do the concepts originate from? How are they *"legal"*?

The Beginning

An important starting point in going beyond stateside asset protection planning is understanding the very origins of our US legal system.

As you are probably aware from your early history lessons, European settlers founded the US. The legal system the early settlers followed had the same British roots that existed in Europe, since they were most familiar with that system. Understanding that the US legal system was founded upon the same legal structure as the British legal system, is an important starting point in understanding how and why going beyond stateside planning is essential for advanced asset protection and wealth preservation planning.

As history evolved in the US, so did the legal system. Much of the basic premises of English, or British common law, continued since this was its roots. In certain court cases within our legal system you will even see the much earlier English cases cited as precedent.

THE FAMILY ASSET PROTECTION TRUST

Founded deeply in the British legal system was the concept of the Family Trust. It was well understood, and accepted basic premise, that assets placed into the Family Trust were not accessible to creditor's claims, unless the Trustee took the necessary steps to collateralize the assets held in the Family Trust. If the Trust Settlor or the beneficiaries of the Family Trust went broke or had claims against them, the assets in the Family Trust could not be touched unless they were earlier collateralized for the benefit of the creditors.

If parties agreed to collateralize assets to provide protection for creditors claims, the assets were reachable and this was fair. However, what's wrong with the concept of holding your non-business or non-investment assets separate from business or collateralized assets? Why shouldn't you be able to place some of your assets, your nest egg, into your unreachable Family Trust, separate and apart from those collateralized business assets?

And too, what happened to the concept that people should

be responsible for their own actions instead of looking for someone else to blame? Why does the fault seem to lie with someone with the deep pocket? Life is not always fair, but why does this mean that the deep pocket defendant should be the one with money ready to dole out, because some idiot was so foolish to spill hot coffee on their lap while driving away from a McDonald's fast food window?

Let me pause for one moment and say that I am not against legitimate creditors rights and claims. I am not in favor of using proper legal tools for purposes of defrauding others. I am against drug dealers and peddlers of sin and other illegal activity that benefit from good, solid legal planning.

But just because there are one or two bad apples in the basket does not mean that we need to toss out the entire bushel. Unfortunately, in an effort to stop certain illegal activities of a few, the rights of a great many in the category of wealth preservation have been greatly sacrificed.

We could write an entire book on the evolution of the sociology and the mentality of the common man and plaintiff lawyer today, motivated by a desire to reach into the pocketbook of others based upon the weakest allegation of wrongdoing. The reality is that this is the environment we live in today, and there is little relief in the foreseeable future.

I have spent two decades of law practice, watching and listening to young lawyers hoping to ring the big bell against a deep pocket defendant, in hopes of enriching themselves in the name of searching for legal rights of an aggrieved plaintiff. It truly makes the stomach turn!

251

U.S. IS NOT BRITISH

While the US adopted the overall concept of English Trust law into its legal system, it made a gradual departure in the category of creditors rights. In our growing industrialized country, the US legal system found reasons why Trust assets could and should be accessible to creditors.

And while departing from the British legal system in the US originally might have had some justification in the early years of the country, by the time the 1960s and 1970s arrived with litigation claims running rampant, it left a gaping hole in the rights of individuals trying to protect and preserve their hard earned assets by using Family Trusts.

Obviously, in the 1800s and 1900s the wild litigation train run amuck in the 1990s and into the 2000s could never have been anticipated. The pendulum swung during the late 1960s and early 1970s from "buyer beware" to "seller-employer-business-owner-professional beware". The unfairness left by the de-

parture from individuals trying to protect and preserve assets was more than obvious. Today this has left a huge hole in the US justice system, where wealth is justifiably transferred daily from one party to another for any number of creative legal reasons.

Your Choice

When there are two common law legal systems that are remarkably similar, that is, the British and US legal systems, why not place your assets under the one that benefits you the most? Does it not make more sense to utilize the British legal system to benefit under Family Trust concepts? Why leave your assets exposed to a US system gone wild, where you and your assets can be separated for a great variety of reasons?

Understanding and accepting that the US, while a great country in many respects, does not have the only legal system in the world, is a first and important step in taking aggressive asset protecting planning for your assets.

Going Offshore-Staying Stateside

Let's get rid of a myth before we go any further. Using the British legal system to your benefit does not necessarily mean expatriating your assets by moving or transferring your assets to distant places on the planet.

While actually transferring your assets offshore is always available to you, there are more desirable options from which to choose. Using the British legal system for your asset protection planning can be accomplished while you retain a reasonable degree of control over your assets.

Before we talk about some of the other locations or jurisdictions, let's look at creating a structure that would help you keep your assets outside of the reach of the money hungry sharks.

Now were getting somewhere!

CHAPTER SIXTEEN

The Structure For Family Asset Protection Trusts

THE CORNERSTONE FOR A FAMILY ASSET PROTEC-tion Trust is establishing the Trust in a British Common-wealth that has enacted strong laws that are specifically designed to protect Trust assets. This does not necessarily mean moving the assets outside of the US, but only establishing the Trust in a different venue.

While the different British Commonwealths around the world all have the same historical English background, where Trusts of this nature have been used for hundreds of years, certain British Colonies have enacted specific statutory legislation which broadens the Trust laws even more.

Chapter Seventeen will identify some of the purposes and

characteristics of the Trust laws. For now it is best that you gain an overview of the basic premises of using a Family Asset Protection Trust. Then, in subsequent chapers, you will see how and why they work.

Transferring Assets

First, an essential part of the goal of protecting and preserving your assets is removing them from the reach of others. To accomplish this you must take the ownership out of your name, and place it in the name of another entity.

You will note that I have chosen the word *ownership*, not the word *control*. While there are control issues to be addressed, for now just think in terms of retitling your assets in the name of another entity in which you retain an important level of control.

Neither you or I should agree to participate in any plan that completely or substantially eliminates control over our assets. There are situations in which you might consider this, but for now, control should essentially remain with you. More on control later.

Avoiding Fraudulent Transfers

Since there are laws designed to prevent fraudulent transfers of assets to avoid existing creditors or lawsuits lurking in the background, you must retitle your assets at a time when you are not confronted with litigation.

As we discussed in Chapter Fifteen, the US legal system is

modeled after British law, with some departures. One such example is that in 1571, the Statute of Elizabeth was adopted in Britain, prohibiting the transfer of assets to delay, hinder, or defraud creditors. In 1924, three hundred and fifty years later, the United Kingdom replaced the Statute of Elizabeth with what eventually became Section 172 of the Law of Property Act of 1925, replacing some restrictions on the earlier Statute of Elizabeth.

Most of the former British Colonies also adopted this change, which defeated the claims of creditors. This latter law became the predecessor for the US legal system, which can be found today in the US Bankruptcy Code, in the Uniform Fraudulent Transfers Act, and in the Uniform Fraudulent Conveyance Act.

If your present intent on transferring assets into a Family Asset Protection Trust is to prevent existing creditors from gaining access to your assets, there are laws that have been around for almost 500 years which are designed to reverse or disregard the transfer altogether.

LEGITIMATE TRANSFERS

I think reasonable people would agree that if you have made obligations to existing creditors, you should satisfy them. But, as long as you have a legitimate business or personal reason other than concealing assets from your present known creditors, then the transfer of assets is viewed differently.

What are some of the legitimate purposes of setting up a Family Asset Protection Trust? One example, is if the device was used as part of an integrated estate plan for your spouse and children after you die, this would generally be considered a legitimate purpose. This is a common goal and easily achieved.

Providing spendthrift provisions for family members is arguably a legitimate purpose as well.

Again, are you thinking synergy?

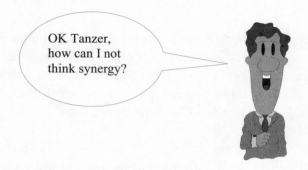

OK Tanzer, how can I not think synergy?

INTEGRATED ASSET PROTECTION PLANNING

Most of the stateside estate planning concepts we discussed in earlier chapters can and should be integrated right into your offshore Family Asset Protection Trust. If your Trust is designed to preserve and protect your assets, why not combine stateside planning with offshore asset protection? The A/B Marital and By-Pass Trusts should be placed right into a section of this Trust called the dispositive provisions. It directs where and how your assets should be disposed of when you die.

Spendthrift provisions can and should be integrated right into the offshore Trust as well. How do you want assets designated for your spouse and children if you die? What type of management and control of the assets do you desire after you die? All of the issues earlier addressed in Section Two can and should be placed into this Trust to accomplish your objectives, during and after your life.

Also, if you are conducting business outside of the US and an offshore entity becomes more convenient than a stateside structure due to local business needs, this might conceivably be a legitimate purpose for the Trust.

Importantly, you should have a purpose for the Family Asset Protection Trust, other than to hide your money or the retitling of assets into the name of new entities that you own or control, which you want to be exempted from the various laws prohibiting fraudulent transfers.

Keep in mind that even the US laws prohibiting fraudulent transfers have a statute of limitations connected with them. In other words, someone making a claim against you must do so within a certain period of time or they are barred from their claim. For example, the US Bankruptcy Code looks back at transfers made over the past 90 days, or one year, depending on the type of transfer.

Even the fraudulent conveyance statutes looks back at transfers made within five or six years. These time periods are important because presumably you cannot have the requisite mental intention to make a fraudulent transfer if you have no present knowledge of a known creditor. It is more or less presumed that you could not have been aware of a new creditor years after the transfer was made.

Many former British Colonies have been aggressively promoting their jurisdictions for the use of Family Asset Protection Trusts. The more aggressive asset protection jurisdictions have reduced the statute of limitations to only one or two years, instead of the longer time periods found in the US. This means that even if you were later found to have made a fraudulent transfer, if a claim against you was not brought in the foreign jurisdiction within one or two years, it would be barred altogether.

THE KEY: ACT NOW

So a claim against you based upon a fraudulent conveyance can be very limited indeed, if the transfer is made in earlier years. The bottom line: you cannot wait until you are presented with a financial catastrophe to retitle your assets, and not expect the transfers to be without problems.

Thus, the first, and one of the most essential rules of establishing a Family Asset Protection Trust is to do it *now* when you are not confronted with creditors claims or pending lawsuits. The second rule: do not forget the first rule and put things off until it is too late.

CONTROLLING YOUR ASSETS

I have used the word *retitling* liberally to get a point across to you. In reality, you are making a conveyance of your assets into a Trust of which you retain a reasonable level of control. Let's see how all of this works.

I have looked at dozens, perhaps hundreds, of different types of structures that fall into the general category of a Family Asset Protection Trust. Different lawyers and promoters have different twists to creating Trusts. Some of their reasons are based upon sound legal and tax purposes, and others are based upon either self-promotion, fees they earn, or connections with particular jurisdictions. Nonetheless, there are certain similarities that can be found with these different structures.

FLP'S & FAPT'S: The Basic Structure

Synergy. Perhaps the most common structure is using a Family Limited Partnership ("FLP") and a Family Asset Protection Trust ("FAPT") founded in the jurisdiction with favorable asset protection laws. Using these two entities together can be very effective at protecting your assets.

You will recall in Chapter Ten we looked at Family Limited Partnerships for stateside asset protection planning. We also discussed the estate planning and tax advantages that could be gained by using this tool. And too, we looked at Family Limited Partnerships in Chapter Fourteen from the aspect of gifting assets, retaining control over the assets, and benefiting from an estate and income tax perspective.

By combining the Family Limited Partnership with an offshore Trust there are far greater benefits you can gain for asset protection planning.

261

By using the FLP you are able to transfer certain assets into this entity and, as General Partner, retain 100% control over those assets. Examples of assets that you would transfer into the FLP include cash, savings accounts, investment funds, C-Corp stock, and other similar investments not having a pass-through tax advantage for the reasons discussed in more detail in Chapters Ten.

The cash accounts, and other investment funds can remain exactly in place as they presently exist. They are merely retitled in the name of the FLP that you control as the 1% General Partner.

As we discussed in earlier chapters, there are numerous ways to hold and own the limited partnership interests.

One of the options in structuring ownership of the partnership interests would be to place the 99% Limited Partnership Interests in the name of a Trust, your Family Asset Protection Trust. The result is that thereafter you only personally own the 1% General Partnership Interest, equal to only 1% of the total value of the assets in the FLP. The remaining 99% of the assets are held in the name of your new Trust. Accordingly, your risk exposure is now limited to 1% of the value of these assets.

Along with owning the 99% interest in the FLP, the Trust could also hold title to certain other assets that have a tax advantage to them. Examples include, S-Corp stock, certain interests in limited liability companies and partnerships. Also, your home or investment real estate, all probably have some tax advantage to you, and these can be transferred to the Trust. Since the Trust is, for US tax purposes, a US Domestic Grantor Trust, these same tax advantages can be passed through directly to you.

The following graph in **Exhibit 16-1** shows how your assets are best transferred for the basic structure:

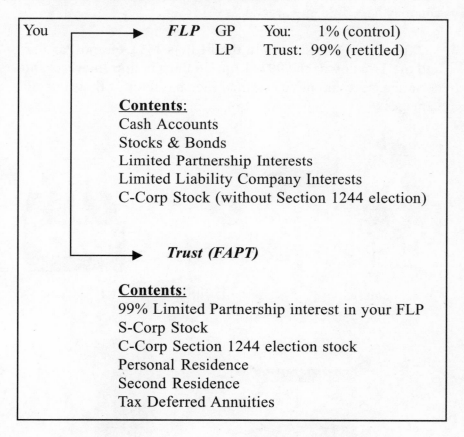

You	*FLP* GP	You:	1% (control)
	LP	Trust:	99% (retitled)

Contents:
Cash Accounts
Stocks & Bonds
Limited Partnership Interests
Limited Liability Company Interests
C-Corp Stock (without Section 1244 election)

Trust (FAPT)

Contents:
99% Limited Partnership interest in your FLP
S-Corp Stock
C-Corp Section 1244 election stock
Personal Residence
Second Residence
Tax Deferred Annuities

SIMPLY STATED

Thus far, you have set up two new entities, a Family Limited Partnership (the FLP) and a Family Asset Protection Trust (the FAPT or the Trust). You have merely retitled, or conveyed, your assets into these entities. The assets are the same assets as before, located at the same local bank if you desire, and have not been relocated or transferred to distant parts of the world as you may have first envisioned.

You control the assets in the FLP as 1% General Partner, and the Trust owns the 99% Limited Partnership Interests and certain assets that have retained the character of their tax advantages.

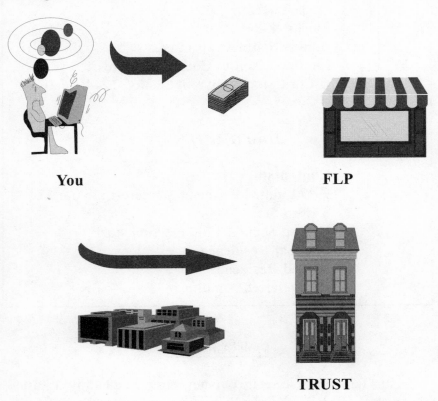

You

FLP

TRUST

264

The Trust

Now, since you have assets held in the name of the Trust, how is the Trust set up and how does it function?

Since Trusts have been around for hundreds of years, you are not creating anything new. But of course, there are some unique provisions in the Trust to make it work as an asset protection tool. Since the Trusts are generally very lengthy and technical, we can only cover some of the more elemental terms, but they should all be well-thought-out for your benefit and to suit your asset and wealth preservation purposes. No two Trusts are exactly alike.

The Trustees

The Family Asset Protection Trust starts with two trustees. One will be a domestic trustee and the other a foreign trustee. The domestic trustee can be a good friend, your brother or business associate, or even a US Trust Company if you like. However, the US Trust Company should be located in an aggressive asset protection state such as Alaska or Nevada.

Importantly, neither you or your spouse should at any time even think about acting as the trustee. The domestic trustee can and will sign documents from time to time associated with the Trust, and is generally able to act independently, upon your direction, without the foreign trustee, if set up properly.

The trustees are the ones that hold what is referred to as "bare legal title" to the trust assets. This means that they do not have any other rights to use or act with respect to the assets other than as set forth in the Trust document, and as long as you do not negate the act. As a practical matter, they can and do only act upon your direction as set forth in the Trust. The authority and power regarding the assets of the Trust must therefore be clearly spelled out in a properly drafted Trust.

The foreign trustee, on the other hand, is located in a jurisdiction which offers more favorable asset protection laws. Generally, you will establish the Trust so that they must also have not only your direction to act, but any act by them with respect to the Trust assets must be accompanied by a signature from the domestic trustee. This gives you an added level of protection by requiring the foreign trustee's signature alongside the domestic trustee's signature, even though the reverse is not required.

Why do you wish to establish two trustees with different signature arrangements? Simple. The first reason is to give you added protection in case you have any doubt of using a foreign trustee located outside of the US. The second reason is that if, and when, a financial calamity arises against you in the US, you can simply terminate the domestic trustee and your foreign trustee is left in place to act according to the Trust terms, and upon your directions consistent therewith. You will see an example of this shortly.

BEYOND U.S. COURT JURISDICTION

In simple terms, you will have another trustee, the foreign trustee, in place that is outside of the jurisdiction of the US legal system. The power of a court in the US does not control the foreign trustee in another jurisdiction. The judge's power is effectively avoided as to the foreign trustee.

The provisions of a well-drafted Trust would include that if there is no longer a domestic trustee, the foreign trustee can act alone, upon your directions. These concepts expand the basic model to Exhibit 16-2.

Exhibit 16-2

BEING PREPARED

What the above dual trustee arrangement does is lay the groundwork for you to act swiftly at a later time if, and when, a financial problem arises. Since you are disciplined enough *now* to establish the Trust at a time when your life is relatively calm and without serious problems, you are not taking any wrongful action.

Remember, these assets belong to you and your family for the purposes set forth in the Trust. When you act *today* to set up the Trust you are taking steps to preserve your assets for the future, with the objectives you establish.

When a calamity hits, as General Partner in the Family Limited Partnership, you, as 1% General Partner, can act immediately to transfer the liquid assets in the FLP outside of the jurisdiction of the US as well, if need be. The foreign trustee could then take over active management of these assets. Up until that point, you have probably kept your liquid assets within the US at your local bank or Money Market Fund, and managed them as you see fit as General Partner of the FLP.

Remember, that since you make the transfer of your assets into the FLP and the Trust *now*, when no catastrophe is present and for legitimate purposes, like estate planning for family members or business reasons, later moving the assets outside of the US and terminating the domestic trustee does not run afoul of the various laws having to do with fraudulent conveyances.

And keep in mind that you will not take this aggressive measure until and unless you are hit with a catastrophe. Until such time, let your money sit right where it is, and later you and the assets are ready to take defensive action.

PLANNING AHEAD

In essence what you are doing is putting a plan in place for rainy days. Think of it as an insurance policy. If you need it and the policy is in place, it's there. However, unlike an insurance policy, you can control it, makes decisions about it, invest it, and not worry about the coverage when you need it most.

Until and unless a financial calamity strikes, you simply go on with your business using the formalities of the structure you established. For example, instead of making a cash deposit or withdrawal in your name, it is in the name of your FLP and you are acting as the General Partner of the FLP. So, in other words, the signature would be David Tanzer, General Partner instead of just David Tanzer. Once in place, it is that simple.

Documentation & Formalities

You will need to follow all other formalities such as documentation of actions taken with respect to the FLP and the Trust, but you will find that this is usually pretty minimal for most people.

For example, if money is transferred from one entity to another, or disbursed to you, you will need to memorialize on paper this event as a loan or distribution to you. Documentation is important to these structures since its demonstrates that you treat them seriously and that they are not just part of your alter ego.

Tax returns need to be filed for both the FLP and the Trust. Income on the FLP is passed through to you on a Schedule K-1 (Form 1065) as the 1% General Partner and 99% to the Trust. Since the Trust is a US Domestic Grantor Trust for tax purposes, the Trust tax return is for informational purposes only and all income is ultimately picked up on your individual tax return. Once these entities are set up and in place, it is much easier than you would imagine.

SUMMARY

As you can see, the basic structure of the Family Asset Protection Trust is relatively clean and simple. You are using the synergy of a Family Limited Partnership, in an aggressive state jurisdiction offering the best protection available, combined with an offshore Trust that can be administered in a British Commonwealth, offering the best Trust law to protect and preserve your assets.

You will soon see how this basic structure can be expanded upon to other levels of protection.

For now, you see the basic structure and how it works. Let's look now at some examples of how it does and does not work, and why. You will then see some examples of how to expand upon this basic structure.

CHAPTER SEVENTEEN

Using the Family
Asset Protection Trust

ONE OF THE GOALS YOU SET OUT TO ACCOM-plish with a Family Asset Protection Trust is to place your assets out of the reach of others, should litigation arise.

Untouchable Assets

Importantly, this objective includes having the option of placing the assets outside of the reach of the US legal system. What good would it be if the US Courts could reach these assets for the benefit of claimants?

A judgment, or court order, from the US is meaningless in

271

most any other jurisdiction. Why? The US courts are a legal part of the US and not a legal part of other countries or their governments. A foreign jurisdiction properly used for asset protection and wealth preservation, would declare that a judgment or order by a US court is without any effect whatsoever.

More significantly, the British Commonwealth of choice would require that any plaintiff actually bring their suit in *their* court system, a cost and burden that will be burdensome on your opponent. And since they will be required to hire a local counsel in that jurisdiction, applying high standards of the British Court is required. Plaintiff's attorney's contingency fees agreements are illegal and not permitted. In essence, you will be placing a very heavy burden upon a paintiff and his attorney in even considering the suit against you in the first place.

Keep in mind that if the claim is against you personally, you have little or no assets, since you have earlier conveyed them into your Family Asset Protection Trust structure. Your opponent simply cannot reach the Trust assets unless they can apply the burdensome fraudulent conveyance statutes in the foreign jurisdiction. Since you dutifully established and transferred your assets into the Trust years earlier, the much shorter statute of limitations in these jurisdictions has probably already expired.

NEGOTIATING FROM A POSITION OF STRENGTH

One of the beauties of having a Family Asset Protection Trust structure in place is that if you are sued, or about to be sued, your attorney can sit down with opposing counsel and lay out right up front, the obstacles they will face if they proceed with their litigation in light of your advanced planning. Oftentimes this alone will generate a quick and easy settlement of pennies on the dollar, since the cost and time will probably not be justified.

For the more persistent plaintiff's legal counsels, time will burn their resources out. Eventually, they will see how difficult and expensive the process really is to proceed against you in trying to reach assets you no longer hold in your name. Eventually, they too will look for a resolution, often for pennies on the dollar.

And if not, they will see that jurisdictions outside of the good old US are not as favorable to parties playing the legal system lottery as we are so accustomed to at home. Their claim will have less opportunity to reward them favorably than they hope for.

Relocating Your Trust

Occasionally it has been asked, what if the country you first select to administer your Family Asset Protection Trust experiences problems of its own. For example, a not so friendly military coup or financial disaster occurs, even though a seemingly remote possibility today. What then of your Trust?

A properly drafted Family Asset Protection Trust will provide you with the authority, as Protector of the Trust, to simply relocate your Trust and reappoint your foreign trustee in another jurisdiction of your choosing. This is an important control which you retain, even though only a secure and long established British Commonwealth jurisdiction is chosen in the first place.

CONTROL

Your control over these vehicles is a very important issue. On one hand, the more control you give up, the easier it is to convince a plaintiff's counsel or the judge that you were serious in the formalities, and the FLP and the Trust had genuine purposes.

On the other hand, the more control you retain, and the more you disregard the formalities of what you set up, the easier it will be for the judge to disregard your structure. So a balance of control is critical.

In a recent, highly controversial case in Nevada, a couple dealt with the very issue of too much control over a Family Asset Protection Trust that they established. The case was highly publicized and became known as the "Anderson" case (F.T.C. v. Affordable Media, LLC, et al, 179 F.3d __ (9th Cir. 1999), 1999 U.S. App. Lexis 13130). This case, even though it arguably has "bad facts" throughout, has set forth an important lesson in how not to act with respect to your Trust. It is also a good lesson in how not to administer a Trust of this type.

The Andersons were involved in a very successful and profitable Ponzi Scheme, where the payment of profits to early investors were available only based upon money paid into the scam by later investors. Their actions were held to be illegal by the judge since it was based upon fraud. Millions of dollars poured in, which the US government claimed was hidden in their Trust in the Cook Islands. The Federal Trade Commission acted to shut them down and have the monies returned to the US. A suit was filed in Nevada, and the judge there ordered the Andersons to return all monies to Nevada.

The Andersons acted as both the domestic trustee and the Protector of their own Trust so that they could retain full power and full control over it. This is certainly not a practice I would recommend for reasons you will soon see.

Only after the judge ordered them to repatriate the money into the US, did the Andersons resign as the US domestic trustees of the Trust. They continued, at least initially, to also act as Protectors under the Trust. The Andersons sent instructions to the foreign trustee in the Cook Islands, to return the money pursuant to the judge's order. The foreign trustee, acting according to the terms of the Trust, properly refused to repatriate monies pursuant to the anti-duress provisions the Andersons had placed in the Trust instrument.

The Andersons then claimed to the court, that they followed the court order the judge issued and that the foreign trustee failed to return the money, therefore, they could not comply with the order of the court. The legal doctrine of "impossibility" is a complete defense to Contempt of Court. But the court noted that the Andersons were the domestic trustees when the order was issued, and they retained the power to determine what events were "duress" as the Protectors, thus, it ordered the Andersons to jail

275

until they complied with the order of court. In other words, the return of the money was not impossible *but for* the events that the Andersons themselves were creating.

The Andersons sat in jail for a short time, since they did not comply with the judge's order. In the meantime, the FTC filed suit in the Cook Islands for the return of the money. The foreign trustee of the Trust in the Cook Islands defended the suit pursuant to the terms of the Trust.

The court in the Cook Islands not only denied the claim of the FTC, but the judge there charged the FTC with paying the Anderson's costs and expenses, including attorney's fees, in defending the suit that it considered improper. A favorable result in the Cook Islands for the Andersons indeed.

The Andersons, in the meantime, were released from jail since they could not possibly comply with the order of court. All said and done, the money remains intact in the Trust established by the Andersons, and the Andersons are freely out and about.

BAD FACTS-GOOD RESULTS?

A good case? Good results? Yes and no.

First, in the opinion of many, including my own, there was a long laundry list of improper Trust planning techniques in the Anderson's situation. They never should have acted as the domestic trustees in the first place and they probably could have avoided the argument that they ultimately retained ownership, the bare legal title, and had complete control of the Trust.

And, the Andersons should have resigned as Protectors of the Trust upon the first clue of any lawsuit against them. Furthermore, proper Protector provisions generally provide the power to control the trustees by having negative powers to overrule any action they take, and by not having positive powers to make decisions as to what is and is not an act of duress, or similar.

The basis of the Anderson's litigation was founded in the fact that they first committed an illegal act that defrauded the general public of millions of dollars, retained too much control over the assets that they acquired, and importantly, created and sustained the very problem of impossibility that they pleaded to the court. That is, by resigning late in the game, they created the impossibility they argued which prevented them from transferring assets back into the US.

On the other hand, the assets remain intact in the Anderson's Trust in the Cook Islands. No funds have ever been touched or repatriated.

Are these desired results? Is it good that the Andersons never lost any money? Is it right that they got away with allegedly defrauding thousands of people in a Ponzi Scheme? Is it good that they spent some time in jail based upon contempt of court? Do you believe that you too would be willing to spend a short time incarcerated in jail if you could protect millions of dollars in your Trust? What price did they pay, and what price are you willing to pay, to protect and preserve assets?

It is often said that bad cases make bad law. The Anderson case is just one more example.

Some uniformed lawyers raised a flag saying that Family Asset Protection Trusts are dead unless you are willing to go to jail. I think not. The true lesson of the Andersons is to make certain that you have a properly drafted Trust in the first place, and be prepared to relinquish control over the Trust as Protector if, and when, you are hit with a financial catastrophe. Being guided by competent legal counsel is very important.

CONTROL OR NOT TO CONTROL

Presumably, you, like most people, have worked long and hard to get where you are financially. The last thing you want to do is give up complete control of your money. You do not need to give up control of your assets. You can, and should, retain sufficient control over the assets in the Trust as the Protector of the Trust, prior to any litigation, and consistent with the Trust terms.

The Protector should retain certain powers over both of the trustees, foreign and domestic, so as to negate any actions you determine should not occur. For example, you could decide that you do not wish that the assets in the Trust be liquidated and gifted to some social cause in a remote part of the world. The type of powers that you, as Protector under the Trust retain, is important for many obvious, and some not so obvious, reasons.

By using the powers of the Protector to give direction and retain rights to negate any actions you might disapprove of is a powerful tool indeed, and gives you the power you need to protect and control the Trust assets. Keep in mind that the purpose of this is to hold technically, the ownership of the assets is in the name of the Trust; that is, the bare legal title is held in the name of the trustees. But as the Protector of the Trust, you can directly, and indirectly, retain sufficient control over the assets prior to any litigation.

But as you saw with the Andersons, control is a dual-edged sword if you are confronted with litigation. Since the Trust is initially designed to allow you to retain control of the assets as Protector of the Trust, if a judge ordered you to repatriate the FLP and Trust assets back into the US, would you have the power to act as Protector? Most arguably so.

Relinquishing Control When Necessary

At the very first hint of the possibility of litigation, you should resign as the Protector of the Trust. At that point, you can establish an agreement with a corporate Protector in a jurisdiction outside of the US to carry out the purposes of the Trust.

Why? This is so a judge within the US jurisdiction cannot order you to act consistent with your powers as Protector and force the assets back into the US. If you retain the powers of the Protector, arguably, the judge can claim you have the powers to act, and therefore do so, or you will be held in contempt of court.

Anti-Duress Clauses

As referenced above, designed into a well-drafted Family Asset Protection Trust is the provision often referred to as an anti-duress clause. This simply means that if you are being *forced* by anyone to give direction to your trustees to act, they can disregard your direction.

For example, if the court ordered you to repatriate those assets and you comply with the court's order by directing the trustees to act, the trustees can simply refuse to comply with your directions since you were forced to do so. Then, since you have complied with the order of court by directing the trustees to send back the money to the good old US, you cannot be held in contempt of court. Technically, it is impossible for you to comply with the order of court. And, you are simply acting consistent with the purpose of the properly established Trust instrument you put into place years earlier.

But if you continued to retain the power of the Protector during litigation, and you could negate the power of the trustee to refuse to comply with the order of court, you would retain too much control. If the foreign trustee simply complies with the Trust provision of ignoring directions pursuant to the anti-duress clause of the Trust that you put in place ages ago, there is no control that you have over the issue.

By resigning as the Protector, you have completely eliminated any control, directly or indirectly, that you retain over the trustees to act in this respect. This is a powerful tool when properly drafted and implemented to protect and preserve your assets.

Interestingly, the anti-duress provisions placed into the Trust are modeled after the provisions put in place in Europe during the 1930 and 1940s. This anti-duress provision founded it roots in the financial desperation of the Jews that were fleeing the jaws of the Hitler regime. Many wealthy Jews held their assets in similar Trusts in Switzerland. The concern was that the Nazi party could force them to provide letters to the trustee, with instructions to return the money from the Trust. The directions in the anti-duress provisions were to ignore the instructions, if the trustees believed it was not the free will of the Protector.

Certainly, any similarity between the Nazi regime and the current US government legal system is not intended.

Oh sure.

Once you resign and assign a new Protector, if the circumstances dictate this extreme action, the new Protector, located in the jurisdiction outside of the US, simply complies with the instructions that they have been given, consistent with the terms of the Trust. You still have your wishes followed and the purpose of the Trust is in place to benefit you and your family, as you first established.

Extraordinary Measures

Keep in mind that the above examples are truly extreme examples of what could happen. It is rare, even when confronted with disastrous litigation.

Most often, by having your structure in place, you can protect your nest egg without nearly as much effort by negotiating a settlement for pennies on the dollar, somewhere along the line. You simply let the plaintiff's counsel know what obstacles he or she faces. In the long run, this is a very important asset protection and wealth preservation technique, since you are preserving not only your assets, but a great deal of money on attorney's

281

fees and costs.

YES, FAPT'S DO WORK!

The bottom line? Family Assets Protection Trusts do work even in extreme circumstances. They are, and will, continue to be tested, occasionally yielding some unusual results.

The true test of a good Family Asset Protection Trust structure is not whether they work absolutely or not, but whether you fare better with them than without them. It is essential that you act with competent and experienced legal advice, and be aware of the obstacles with which you might be confronted.

Let's now look closer at various jurisdictions and the benefits that they offer you, before we go into examples of expanding the basic structure of Family Asset Protection Planning.

CHAPTER EIGHTEEN

Selecting the Right Jurisdiction

D IFFERENT BRITISH COLONIES OFFER DIFFERENT advantages for your Family Asset Protection Trust. There is not a one size fits all program. Your particular needs will dictate which jurisdiction you should elect in which to set up your Family Asset Protection Trust and designate a foreign trustee.

No one place is best for everyone.

AVOIDING U.S. PRESSURE

It is important that you avoid jurisdictions that are vulnerable to pressure from the United States or the United Kingdom.

This is becoming increasingly difficult to do. The US continues to exert pressure on many territories under the name of drug enforcement and money laundering. While these are noble pursuits, the implications of these laws can reach way beyond the bad guys to good people like you and me. The more these countries compromise confidentiality and bow to US pressure, the less attractive they become for purposes of wealth preservation.

The countries more vulnerable to these risks are countries under direct control of the United Kingdom. Some of the last outposts of the British Empire include the Channel Islands, Anguilla, Bermuda, British Virgin Islands, Cayman Islands, Gibraltar, Isle of Man, Jersey, Montserrat, and the Turks and Caicos Islands. These territories have varying degrees of asset protection laws, even though they are popular and recognizable names. Importantly, there can often be too much control exercised over them by the UK.

Former independent British Colonies which are founded upon the English system, are generally better based upon the criteria of similarities in the legal systems.

AVOIDING ENFORCEMENTS OF U.S. JUDGEMENTS

Obviously, you should avoid jurisdictions that enforce foreign judgments or have tax treaties with the US, which report your US investments. Unfortunately, the US has made tremendous headway in this respect through the use of tax treaties and the like.

For example, while Switzerland has been well-known as a strong worldwide banking leader with strong confidentiality requirements, it has still buckled under US pressures of recognizing foreign judgments, and even disclosing account information under certain circumstances. While it is a great banking community, it is not well-known for asset protection planning. The same is probably true for Barbados.

Switzerland, along with other certain banking communities, has entered into a bilateral tax treaty with the US, agreeing to report investments made by their US clients in US securities. The effective dates have been postponed several times, but the application of this reporting to the IRS is all but certain.

The only alternative left for US investors is to not hold US securities through institutions agreeing to these reporting requirements, and instead invest in non-US securities. Keep in mind that these reporting requirements apply to honest citizens not intending to evade reporting income, and who only desire privacy in their personal affairs. Big brother will be watching.

Pro-Active Trust Law

Some jurisdictions have taken a hard-nosed stance against US intrusion into their internal affairs and actively enact legislation for individual asset protection. The purpose of the statutory revisions contained in the individual commonwealths are to actually promote the use of the jurisdiction for the establishment of Family Asset Protection Trusts.

Other jurisdictions have been more aggressive in marketing their jurisdictions than others, and several US lawyers and Trust promoters have actually assisted in the drafting of the revised statutory Trust laws, to help facilitate the establishment of a Trust in a particular jurisdiction.

AVOID SPECIAL PROMOTERS

The statutory Trust provisions in a particular British Commonwealth location can vary, as well as the services offered by a particular Trust company. Depending on your goals, one jurisdiction might be better for you than another. I suggest you not use an attorney that limits his or her work to only one company in one jurisdiction, since he or she is probably more interested in promoting their own interest, than in working to protect yours.

While the field of attorneys and companies offering services of this nature around the world is still relatively small, it is growing. Coming with that growth is more competitive pricing and a greater availability of services.

OTHER FACTORS

An important key factor in selecting a country to establish a Trust should be based upon low or no taxes. Political stability of the government is also essential. As noted above, avoid bilateral or multi-lateral tax treaties in mutual cooperation with the US, where your privacy could be jeopardized. Jurisdictions with a history of no currency restrictions and minimal governmental intrusions is critical.

Communications and availability of local legal counsel and other professional services are all-important factors as well. Having familiarity with the legal system and the language is important. Also, the jurisdiction should be reasonably accessible to travel, unless you are a masochist.

Reprinted with special permission of King Features Syndicate

SELECTED JURISDICTIONS

In alphabetical order, here are some of the more important asset protection jurisdictions that have been used:

287

Anguilla is a small island with a population of around 10,000 residents, east of the British Virgin Islands. The weather is very pleasant and English is spoken. Communications are good and accessibility is fair.

Unfortunately, there is question about the privacy provision and little confidence that foreign judgments will be ignored. There is a minimal standard of proving a fraudulent conveyance, a longer statute of limitations related to transfers, and other short-comings in general related to asset protection Trust laws. This community is generally not regarded as a good asset protection jurisdiction.

The **Bahamas** is one of the best known of the traditional tax havens located only 50 miles off the U.S. coast of Florida. The Bahamas is an independent country and a member of the British Commonwealth. It is a crown jewel indeed, and one of the most stable governments in the Caribbean. The official language is English, the Bahamian dollar is maintained on par with the US, and there are no exchange controls. Bahamas has no tax treaty with the US.

While not necessarily the best, it is *"better in the Bahamas"* for a variety of reasons. Banking, International Business Corporations ("IBC") and life insurance investments are popular investment vehicles as tools to own or protect assets, and they get a huge thumbs-up in this regard. The infrastructure is very good and growing.

In 1990, laws were implemented allowing for Bahamian residency and a passport based upon an investment in that country. However, like Anguilla, the Bahamas has too many shortcomings with its present Trust laws to be regarded as a good jurisdiction for asset protection planning.

As far as banking or use of offshore insurance products, the Bahamas offer great opportunities. And too, I must say that I have a great respect for the Bahamian attitude towards US attempts to interfere in their political and legal system. On a recent visit to the Bahamas I met with the Honorable Darrel E. Rolle, a retired Cabinet Minister of some of the most sensitive Ministries in the Bahamas. He summarized the general sentiment of the government in seven simple words: *"The US government can go screw themselves."* Now that's international policy hard at work!

The Latin American Country of **Belize,** formerly known as British Honduras, is a recent contender to the asset protection world. This is a small independent country on the Caribbean, southeast of Mexico and north of Honduras. The language is English and the currency is based upon the dollar. Communications are good. In the past, there was some blatant abuse by government officials offering second passports.

Presently they have a very aggressive campaign to attract wealthy retirees by offering extended tax and import duty holidays with the lure of a sound, second passport for a relatively nominal fee. There are over 10,000 registered International Business Corporations ("IBC") in Belize, the largest in the world behind only the Caymans, British Virgin Islands and Bahamas.

In the past, the Trust laws for asset protection planning were mediocre. However, over the past several years, they have gotten far more aggressive in trying to encourage Trust and Banking in their community and have taken steps in this regard. While the recent developments in this territory are very good for a worldwide provider of asset protection and banking services, I still believe that it is a bit too early to tell, and I would recommend a wait and see attitude.

The **British Virgin Islands** ("BVI's") are also a well-known group of islands located in the Caribbean. They are independent and follow English Common Law. Currency is based upon the US dollar, and tax is only based upon income earned on the islands. The reporting requirements are nominal. Infrastructures, business and legal services are excellent, and communications and accessibility are good.

The BVI's have also enacted specific asset protection laws, founded upon the Cook Islands, but they are not as comprehensive as the Cook Island legislation, even though they have strict secrecy laws in place. While a great community for an IBC, they are still lacking in regards to being recognized as a top quality asset protection jurisdiction due to the higher standards found in the Cook Islands and in Nevis.

The **Cayman Islands** are another well-known group of islands just south of Florida. Although there is a form of tax on Trust income, there is a tax holiday that you can obtain for up to 50 years. The banking and Trust and insurance business is big in the Caymans. The Caymans have also implemented legislation to benefit asset protection planning, although it is not seen as being as aggressive as some of the other territories discussed here. And too, there are a number of shortcomings in their asset protection Trust laws, namely enforcing foreign judgments, standards for establishing fraudulent transfer intentions, and retention of control by Settlors of the Trust.

The **Channel Islands** are located off the coasts of France and England. Since the ties are too close to England, they are not seen as a good asset protection jurisdictions. I have heard that it is a nice place to visit.

The **Cook Islands** are located off the coast of New Zealand and are one of the best jurisdictions for Family Asset Protection Trusts. These are independent and self-governing islands, with the law originally based upon English law. The language is English. The Trust laws in the Cooks were drafted, in part, by a group of US lawyers from Denver, along with a Barrister named Reuben Tylor who lives in the Cooks. In the late 1980's they sought, and succeeded, in creating the most aggressive asset protection territory in the world.

By all practical accounts, the Cook Islands are probably the very best for asset protection planning type of Trusts. There are several well-qualified Trust Companies located in the Cooks that I have dealt with, and the communications system between the US and the Cooks is considered reasonable.

The statutory trust laws are excellent in the Cooks. The government is very solid and stable. Privacy laws are strict. Worthy of note is that Asiaciti Trust, one of the Cook Islands Trust companies, defended the litigation in the Anderson case originating in Las Vegas, Nevada that I spoke about earlier. They did an excellent job fighting the deep pockets of the US FTC, thanks to the leadership of the General Manager and Australian Barrister Adrian Taylor and the Executive Chairman, Graeme Briggs.

Costa Rica is perhaps one of my favorite places in the world to visit. The literacy rates are higher than in the US, and the medical system is just as good but, less expensive. The people are very polite and formal, and there is a great respect towards

North Americans, as long as you demonstrate a respect towards them. Communications and accessibility is good, and there is a fair infrastructure and availability of business and legal services.

However, it is a Civil Law system, not a common law system, and offers little benefits for asset protection planning. While Costa Rica itself is considered stable, there have been boundary disputes with its neighbor to the north, Nicaragua, and some concern, of drugs and violence spilling over from the south borders. Otherwise, this is truly a gem of a country and hopefully they will be able to eliminate some of the problems that presently plague Latin America.

Gibraltar is a small British Colony located at the tip of Spain. An interesting difference about the law enacted in Gibraltar is that it does not focus on the intent of the parties when establishing a Trust, instead looking at the balance sheet and solvency of the party setting it up. While there are several Trust Companies in this jurisdiction, it is still controlled by the UK and generally not considered a strong asset protection territory.

Grenada is probably best known for the US invasion in which our troops came to the rescue of US medical students. This little island country is not at all known for asset protection planning, as a tax haven, or for banking or insurance products. However, what makes Grenada worthy of mention is that recently it has enacted a very liberal second passport and citizenship program for a reasonable price. Dual citizenship and another passport to travel to parts of the world where US citizenship is actually detrimental, is worth considering. Chapter Twenty One looks into some of these issues closer.

Hong Kong is one of the largest financial centers in the world, following London and New York. Tax is only imposed on income earned in Hong Kong. While Hong Kong was formally a British Colony, China has taken over this territory. There are many uncertainties with using this jurisdiction and it is presently not very favorable.

Liechtenstein is a small country next to Switzerland and is probably best known as a banking center rather than an asset protection center. One of its benefits over Switzerland is that the banking secrecy laws are probably stronger.

Madeira is a civil law country and one of the Portuguese Colonies. English is widely spoken. However, since Trusts are based upon common law principals, and Madeira is a civil law system, it took a very creative approach in attempting to create Trust Law. Madeira applied strong asset protection concepts from multiple jurisdictions which is favorable, and may prove to be a diamond in the rough. Nonetheless, I am unaware of much serious use of this jurisdiction.

The Caribbean Island of **Nevis**, second only to the Cook Islands, is probably one of the best asset protection jurisdictions in the world. It is considered politically and financially stable. The Trust Law is closely modeled after the Cook Islands, known as the best asset protection law. The legislation works. Reporting requirements are minimal. The language is English.

While the development in Nevis is still minimal, there is a great Four Seasons Resort that has invested a large sum of money into the local system. Nevis, like Belize and Grenada, has a good second passport program, but it is much more costly. One of the

293

benefits it has over the Cook Islands is that it is closer to the US, if you feel compelled to visit your foreign trustee. But there are still no easy flight connections to Nevis, which may be a deterrent to your opposing counsel.

Nevis and the Cook Islands are my favorite choices in which to establish a Family Asset Protection Trust.

St. Vincent is another strong contender for asset protection laws. The language is English. There are zero taxes on IBCs. Privacy is a premium. The major Trust Company is formed in Liechtenstein, which requires it to operate more with European standards than Caribbean standards. While it appears to be another good alternative, I am not aware of many lawyers using this jurisdiction, for whatever the reasons might be. Perhaps time will reveal these reasons to be minimal leaving St. Vincent as a future possibility.

Switzerland has long been recognized as a true banking haven. Secrecy laws are strongly enforced. Swiss bankers are respected worldwide for their knowledge and proficiency. However, as noted earlier, the US has made inroads into this veil of privacy and Switzerland has not been looked upon as a strong asset protection jurisdiction.

Nonetheless, its banking standards have set the model for other jurisdictions around the world, and the Swiss banker is second to none. The banks in the Bahamas take great effort to point out that many are owned or controlled, or at least follow, the high standards of the Swiss banker.

Swiss investment bankers treat their customers like royalty. You first make an appointment with your personal banker. When you arrive at the entrance to the Bank, you are greeted in the lobby by a receptionist who discreetly informs your personal banker that you have arrived and summons the elevator for you. When the elevator opens at your floor, your private banker is there to welcome your presence and immediately escorts you to a personal and private conference room. He or she will spend as much time with you as necessary, to assist with your banking and investment needs.

However, keep in mind that you cannot just walk into a reputable Swiss Bank and open an account. *"Know thy Customer"* is an important element in banking policy with Swiss bankers. They can, and will, do without your business.

Most relationships with top quality investment advisors come from a referral from another professional or the bank's clientele. Obtaining topnotch quality services generally requires opening an account with minimum balances of around $200,000 or more. However, you can often open mutual funds accounts for much less, that do not require or receive such personal attention.

As you can see by the above brief examples, there are numerous competitors looking to assist you with your asset protection needs. The cost for services, or to establish and maintain a Trust, varies considerably. Of particular importance is making certain that the Trust Company is well-established, insured, has experienced personnel and management, and is backed by reputable owners.

Dealing with the Trust Company

The above is only a partial listing of what is available; an entire book could be written expanding on the above options. As I noted above, the Cook Islands are my first choice for an asset protection jurisdiction, and Nevis is my second, due to the Trust law, stable jurisdiction, and availability of solid Trust Companies with experienced people.

For all practical purposes, how much contact do you generally have with a foreign trustee? Very little.

When a Trust is first established, you communicate with them through your legal planner as to how you wish to establish it, and the formalities you desire to achieve the goals. Then, your legal counsel sends the package off for their signature on the Trust documents and awaits their return. Once a year you will pay them an annual fee between $1,500 and $2,200 (more or less depending on the company, jurisdiction and services provided). On a general-use basis, there is not much more involvement on their part except for an occasional execution of a document.

Then, when you need to convey assets out of the Trust or have Trust informational tax returns signed, you can have the domestic trustee sign and return them, instead of using the foreign trustee. You probably took note of the fact that the type of assets placed into the Trust are not assets that are typically bought and sold on a routine annual basis, so the burden on your domestic trustee is pretty small.

DEALING WITH THE CATASTROPHE

The essential part of your asset protection plan waits until you need to take action. If, and when, you are hit with a financial catastrophe, you can take action with Plan B to your Masterplan. Remember that the time to shop for a life raft is not when the boat is sinking.

At the first hint of a lawsuit against you, immediately fire your domestic trustee. Then, you, as General Partner of your FLP, can transfer liquid assets already placed into the FLP, to a banking jurisdiction outside of the US.

You and your foreign trustee can also consider if there is a need and legitimate purpose to take out mortgages on Trust real estate with equity. If so, the real estate can immediately be collateralized with a back-to-back loan. That is, your foreign trustee obtains a loan on the Trust real estate secured by a mortgage, placing the proceeds of the loan into a savings account offshore. The real estate is then fully encumbered and no longer a target of your creditors.

Since you already made the conveyances into your FLP and into the Trust years earlier when litigation was not a concern, you avoid fraudulent conveyances today, and subsequent creditors now arriving on the scene have no rights to these assets.

Significantly, since you established these vehicles and the structure of your Trust long ago with legitimate purposes in mind, you are not acting illegally when assets are moved around to protect them. There cannot be any valid claims of fraudulent transfers, since if the claim is against you personally, not the FLP or the Trust, what the Family Limited Partnership or the Trust does is irrelevant. They are simply acting to fulfill the Trust purposes of asset and wealth preservation.

The only exposure to any of your assets is the 1% general partnership interest you retained to manage the FLP.

THE BOTTOM LINE

Here is where the foreign trustee finally comes into play. Since you terminated the domestic trustee upon the first clue of a financial catastrophe, you will now rely upon the services of the foreign trustee. The professionalism of the foreign trustee will be essential when you are forced to take these aggressive measures.

Having confidence that they can and will perform is essential, since they will now need to execute your plan. The discount service provider with limited experience is of little value in protecting your assets when lighting strikes.

Now that you have seen how the basic structure works and looked at what some of the different jurisdictions can offer, let's take a closer look at expanding these aggressive asset protection planning techniques.

CHAPTER NINETEEN

Expanding the Basic Planning Structure

I N CHAPTER EIGHT WE EXPLORED THE DIFFERENT entities that can be used to conduct your business, and the importance of using these to limit your exposure. You will recall with the example of Mr. Chuckly we explored creating multiple entities. In his situation, and with good tax planning by his CPA's, Mr. Chuckly increased the overall value of his business and also saved on taxes.

SEGREGATING ASSETS

The concept with Family Asset Protection Trust structures is somewhat similar to Mr. Chuckly's pool and spa business. In other words, if some protection is good, then more protection is probably better. Let's look at some possibilities as to how the basic Family Asset Protection Trust can be expanded.

Mr. Martin owns a successful lounge and restaurant at the bottom of the ski slopes in Vail known for outstanding "apres ski", known as "The Spot". For obvious reasons the names have always been changed in this book. For the non-skier types, apres ski means being at a gathering place following a great day on the mountain where you can indulge in food and drink and meet some of those interesting bodies that can be seen on the ski-mountain during the day.

The Martins, a young couple with two young children, were worth between $2,000,000 and $3,000,000 at the time they structured their asset protection planning. They had strong prospects of increasing their wealth in the future, due to appreciation and good asset management objectives.

Mr. Martin started The Spot about a decade ago, and it has literally turned into a cash cow for him. Instead of living lavishly and consuming his income, he has invested it wisely. He now owns about 12 different commercial and residential investment properties and a comfortable nest egg in several money market funds.

THE GOAL

Mr. Martin's greatest concerns are that liability extending

from the bar or the commercial properties could wipe out his wealth with just one mishap.

Before I first assisted the Martins with reaching their asset protection objectives, their asset holding structure was as set forth in Exhibit 19-1. You can see that no asset protection planning occurred other than placing the restaurant and bar into a corporation, which itself had problems due to corporate formalities not kept in compliance.

Exhibit 19-1

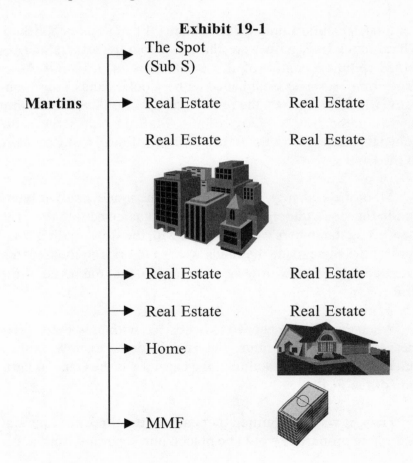

The Spot
(Sub S)

Martins

Real Estate   Real Estate

Real Estate   Real Estate

Real Estate   Real Estate

Real Estate   Real Estate

Home

MMF

THE RESULT

The Spot was already placed in an S Corp and the couple together owned their home and all of the other investment real estate and funds individually. After considerable review of tax issues related to The Spot and their investment properties, and a review of goals that Mr. Martin and his family sought to accomplish, an expanded version of the basic structure for the Family Asset Protection Trust was used.

First, a Family Limited Partnership ("FLP") was established, where he and his wife were the 1% General Partners and retained complete control of all cash and stocks. A Family Asset Protection Trust was established with a Cook Islands Trust company, which would own the remaining 99% Limited Partnership interest in the FLP. A relative of Mrs. Martin would serve as the domestic trustee, with the foreign trustee of the Trust Company in the Cooks.

All of the cash personally owned in the money market funds and in the stock trading accounts were transferred into the FLP. New account numbers were assigned with the stock trading company at the same place the funds were held prior to the transfer. The trading company now held the accounts in the name of the FLP.

When the Martins needed to deposit or withdraw funds from these accounts in the future they would do so exactly as they had in the past, except acting in the capacity as the General Partners of the FLP.

Then, it was determined that each of the three commercial real estate properties would be placed into separate Limited Liability Companies with the Trust as the owner. It was believed that the potential for liability, for example a slip and fall or similar accident, was greater with commercial property. So if liability arose out of any one of the commercial investments, the exposure and risk would be limited to the assets of the individual Limited Liability Company and not expose any of the other Trust assets. Since the Limited Liability Company was a single member ownership that is owned by the Trust, all tax advantages passed through the Trust and to Mr. and Mrs. Martin.

The residential investment property was believed by the Martins to be in a much lower risk category for a variety of reasons. It was also part of a short-term plan in which some of these investments would be liquidated in the very near future. With those ideas in mind, it was decided that all residential investment property would be placed into one separate single member Limited Liability Company owned by the Trust. Tax benefits similarly passed through to the Trust and to the Martins.

Most accountants will note that no partnership income tax returns are required for the LLC due to the single member status. However, for asset protection planning reasons, it is recommended that an informational tax return be filed, demonstrating additional efforts of separate accounting for each LLC.

The Spot nightclub was a little trickier since it was placed in an S-Corp. owned by Mr. Martin. There were a number of tax issues that had to be considered. While Mr. Martin runs a great apres-ski club, he was not very proficient in keeping up with corporate formalities.

The corporate formality issues were addressed, and ultimately it was decided with advice from good outside tax advisors, that

303

keeping The Spot in an S-Corp, owned in the name of a Trust, was the best method. Any liability would remain within the S-Corp, as long as the formalities were properly satisfied.

The revised asset protection structure is set forth in Exhibit 19-2. This structure is very similar to the basic structure you saw in Chapter 18, except that it is now expanded upon, using multiple entities for holding the various investments and the restaurant and bar. Again, the goal for these multiple entities is to keep any exposure to risk and liability to the one asset, or group of assets, separate from all other assets owned by the Martins.

This is synergism at its best:

Exhibit 19-2

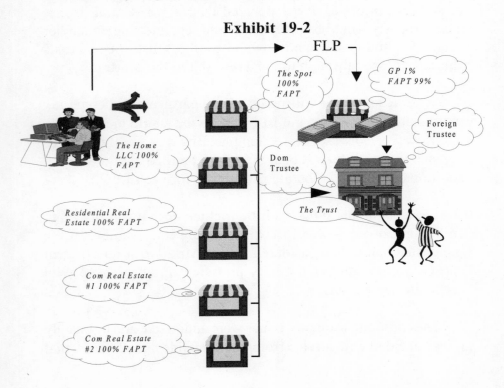

How it Works

With the above asset protection structure in mind, you can now see that the cash and stocks in the FLP are controlled by Mr. and Mrs. Martin in their capacity as General Partners, and the exposure to the risk and liability from other assets is segregated. The potential for liability and risk generated by The Spot was limited to the S-Corp structure.

Since each of the commercial real estate investments were contained within their own structure, the potential risk and liability was limited to the equity of each separate structure.

The residential investment real estate, with lower liability concerns for the Martins, was limited to the equity alone in those properties. I was personally concerned that any one of the residential investment properties could create liability similar to the commercial properties, and therefore recommended separate Limited Liability Companies for each investment for the best attainable protection.

As an alternative, I recommended that if the residential properties were not each placed into their own Limited Liability Company, then to divide them up into perhaps two or three separate companies instead of just one.

However, due to the use of leveraged loans and the near term objectives of selling some of the real estate, the Martins decided to place all of the residential investment into one entity. When any one real estate was sold, the cash would go into the FLP. If any one real estate was held long term and substantial equity was in any property, it could then be placed into a sepa-

305

rate Limited Liability Company.

The Martin's primary residence was placed into a separate single member Limited Liability Company, with the Trust being the sole member. This would allow the Martins to benefit from tax regulations while they owned the property or upon its sale. In the interim, the home was a segregated entity for asset protection purposes.

The Martins also decided to establish a separate Child's Trust for their young children. Annual spousal gift giving in amounts of $20,000.00 for each child would fund each Child's Trust and these amounts and the growth would be kept separate and apart from all other assets. An outline of goals and distributions was listed in the Child's Trust, and restrictions on distributions were made based upon each child accomplishing specific goals.

INTEGRATED PLANNING

Not to forget estate planning objectives, the Trust held all of the dispositive provisions for the Martins. It included an A/B Marital By-Pass Trust which would make the first $2,000,000 of their assets non-taxable, as of 2006.

Since Mr. Martin had also established a life insurance policy with a value of $500,000, it was important that this be removed from his estate to save taxes. A new life insurance policy, at substantial savings, was established and placed in an Irrevocable Life Insurance Trust. His wife and children were named as beneficiaries.

The estate tax savings for the Martins were substantial. Depending on asset valuations and gift giving to the Child's Trust, the present day estate tax savings was estimated somewhere between $500,000 and $1,000,000 overall, assuming certain existing and anticipated future conditions were met. This was a significant source of wealth preservation when viewed that the Martins desired to pass as much to their children as they could when they passed away.

Liability insurance was still maintained on the nightclub, commercial real estate and residential real estate. But the costs for insurance were a big savings too since they decided to increase the deductibles, and did not believe that they needed to carry the large coverage amounts for so many categories of liability as they did earlier. This alone was a big cash flow benefit to them.

Most importantly, Mr. and Mrs. Martin had the peace of mind that they had outstanding asset protection planning in place.

PLANNING AHEAD

What steps would the Martins take if someone in the future tried to sue them and challenge the structure they created today?

Simple. As General Partners, the Martins would have reinvested their cash and stocks into good solid banks or investment companies located outside of the US. This would mean that no one could tie these funds up seeking unfair leverage over the assets. Either the Martins as General Partners of the FLP or the foreign trustee could assume management of these funds pursuant to the terms of the Trust instrument.

When sued, the Martins would terminate their domestic trustee and benefit more fully from the services of their foreign trustee in the Cook Islands. If necessary, the equity in the real estate could be fully mortgaged by taking out a new loan in the amount of the equity, collateralized by the real estate, and then reinvesting that cash into a savings account outside of the US.

Since the asset protection structure was created and funded at a time when there was no adversity in their lives, the Martins would have minimal concerns as to challenges of fraudulent conveyances. And even if this was challenged, they knew that the Cook Islands have one of the best Trust laws worldwide, greatly limiting challenges of this nature.

The above measures would permit the Martins to fairly and reasonably level the playing field with their adversaries. Concerns of being wiped out entirely were significantly reduced. As the Andersons discovered in the Las Vegas, Nevada litigation, there is never a 100% guarantee on anything, but the Martins were now in a far stronger position to resolve litigation during the negotiation process should a catastrophe arise.

In the case of litigation, the Martin's own counsel would early on size up the claim and their potential exposure. Was the claim collateralized or covered by insurance? Was there an opportunity to resolve matters early in the process saving significant time, money and aggravation? What was the plan? What are the alternatives? What are the risks and the exposure?

Then, disclosing to opposing counsel the structure and legitimate purpose that the Martin's Family Asset Protection Trust was created for, makes it clear that it will not be an easy challenge for the plaintiff and its counsel to break into.

A wise plaintiff's lawyer will eventually size matters up and realize that the big battle might best be left for another day, or a weaker adversary. A foolhardy lawyer might proceed for awhile, but will probably make a lot of loud noise, which in due time would probably subside and allow for better judgment to prevail.

Outlining the structure and the related challenges to opposing counsel will allow the Martins to negotiate a settlement from a position of strength. The time to reach a settlement is not when you are at the mercy of others, but when you can speak with confidence from a stronger position than your opponent. This is a basic premise of effective negotiation and reaching fair settlements.

Importantly, as noted earlier, the success or failure of your asset protection planning should not be measured by whether you win or lose a particular dispute, or whether you had to part with some of your assets. The key measuring stick is whether or not you fared better with your asset protection structure than if you did not have it at all.

In other words, if the planning provided you with at least some reasonable degree of protection and preservation of your assets, this is a success. Of course, some wish to take the greatest degree of protection to minimize their risk and therefore seek as many alternatives, using the synergy that they offer, to find the highest level of protection available.

Creative legal structuring of assets and removing assets from

309

a legal jurisdiction beyond your creditors reach, is only left to your imagination, based upon your goals.

CREATIVE STRUCTURING

Are there more things that you can do to expand upon the Family Asset Protection Trust structure to help you protect and preserve your assets? You bet! Based upon earlier concepts in this book, can you think of a few?

Several other options should quickly come to mind. First, remember we discussed the opportunity to use Family Limited Partnerships for gifting purposes. You will recall that you have an opportunity to discount the value of the Limited Partnership interests and gift them to your children while you retain control. The structure also offers a first level of asset protection planning.

If it was within the objectives of the Martins, they could have created a second or third Family Limited Partnership. Instead of having the Trust own the 99% interest in all of the FLPs, they could have retained all interest in one themselves, both as General Partners and Limited Partners. Then they could have placed one or more of the different investment real estate properties into the FLP and by discounting, could have given up to $15,000 annual gifts to each of their children, each year, with aggressive gift planning.

Contrary to my recommendations to the Martins, they elected not to follow my advice and create additional individual Limited Liability Companies for each of the residential investment properties. They reasoned that they intended to sell off some of these properties in the near future, and liability was a lesser concern.

If you intend to hold onto investment real estate for a longer term creating greater equity, you should give consideration to placing each property into a separate entity, or at least breaking them out so that many eggs are not in the same basket.

Another consideration would be to segregate the home from the Trust assets altogether.

What are the Trust assets when the restructuring of the Martin assets was completed? The Trust owned the Limited Liability Company that owned the home, the Sub-S nightclub, the Limited Liability Company for each of the commercial real estate investments, and the Limited Liability Company for all of the residential real estate as you saw in Exhibit 19-2. What if the formalities of any one of the entities were not properly kept up and a claimant pierced the veil of any one of these? Or, what if the Trust was sued because it was functioning in a capacity that generated liability (although this activity is strongly discouraged)?

In the above situations, the Trust assets could all be exposed to claimants. Does this mean the Trusts are useless? Hardly! It simply means that formalities and structures must be followed and properly documented.

An extra level of precaution could also be created using multiple Trusts, to hold different types of properties with different goals. Each structure would stand on its own and help to demonstrate that these structures each had their own purposes, and

311

would lend to help you with even a greater level of asset protection planning and wealth preservation.

THE IBC

Another use of aggressive asset planning includes using an International Business Corporation (an "IBC"), instead of a US corporation, to own domestic or foreign real estate. While there are IRS reporting requirements of foreign owned corporations and passive income derived from these corporations, they still offer a great opportunity to create more obstacles in your litigation happy opponent's path.

The British Virgins Islands, the Bahamas, and other countries, have long been recognized for aggressive use of IBC structures. The initial capitalization amounts and reporting requirements are generally very nominal.

You can use an IBC to own property inside or outside of the US. Attempting to gain information on who owns real estate, for example, and how, is difficult and sometimes impossible when owned by an IBC. What better method to help confuse the suit happy plaintiff?

Proper tax planning using this tool is critical, since there are burdens on reporting the IBC and income to the IRS. You can also run into tax issues that make them more burdensome to use than planned. But as long as you acknowledge to the IRS the entity, and take the necessary steps to satisfy tax issues, the IBC is a great asset protection and wealth preservation tool.

Reporting Requirements

A list of current reporting requirements for US citizens investing globally and utilizing offshore Trusts is outlined at the end of the book in Appendix A. While all forms will not be required under each structure that you create, you and your advisors should certainly be aware of the different forms and remain compliant. Do not be put off by the long list; simply be a knowledgeable US citizen and avoid IRS problems.

While offshore Trusts and other asset planning tools are slightly more complex than the KISS method (Keep it Simple Stupid), if you are serious and hire a competent attorney, they certainly afford you a very aggressive asset protection and wealth preservation strategy.

Cover Thy Assets

Like anything else, Family Asset Protection Trusts can be abused. Creditors do have rights too, and this should not be ignored. But the pendulum has swung so far to the left in the US with suit happy plaintiffs and their hungry lawyers ready to take on the smallest of disputes in hopes for quick and easy settlements. You could be next.

But, just because there is one bad apple in the entire cart that might take advantage of the Family Asset Protection Trust structure, does not mean that we should stop growing apples. There is certainly a strong case to go back to our English roots and openly and legally allow a simple domestic Family Trust be created in the US, that prohibits creditors from reaching the assets placed into the Family Trust, unless they are specifically

313

collateralized. Why is this unfair?

Forcing individuals to be more responsible for themselves, realizing that some bad things do unfortunately happen in life, would be relief to an already over-burdened legal system. But unfortunately, this mentality and return to civility has little promise of happening in our lifetime.

Taking aggressive measures to protect your assets is the next best choice to changing humanity.

Finally, can owning your own bank serve as a method to help protect and preserve your assets? Is this a realistic opportunity? Do you need to be really rich to do this? Read on.

CHAPTER TWENTY

Your Own Offshore Bank

MANY INVESTORS TODAY CONDUCT THEIR business or own property outside the boundaries of the US for legitimate business purposes. The laws are often different outside of the US, and rules of conducting business can be very different.

As noted in Chapter 19, oftentimes owning an International Business Corporation ("IBC") to hold assets inside or outside of the US, is desirable for legitimate business purposes as well as for asset preservation goals. The same is true of owning your own bank outside of the US.

I know it all has something to do with that synergy stuff.

OWNING THE BANK

Why is owning an International Bank an asset protection tool? How does it work? How much money do you need to start your own bank? Is it complicated? Are there compliance issues you must meet as a US citizen owning an International Bank?

These are all good questions which we will explore one by one.

But first, several caveats are in order since there are pitfalls in owning an international bank. Owning an offshore bank is for someone experienced in banking, someone willing to invest their time and money in becoming knowledgeable in banking, or someone with the ability to hire the right management team to operate the bank. While these requirements will eliminate many potential "offshore bankers", to those select few under the right circumstances, owning an offshore bank can be highly profitable in the world of offshore investing and asset protection planning.

Remember that a basic premise of this book is that you have a fundamental and legal right to do what you wish with your assets, including the right to protect and preserve them. Good solid asset protection techniques in the US are becoming increasingly difficult. As you see in Appendix A, the reporting requirements for investing outside of the US and using offshore techniques are full of potential problems if you do not fill out the bureaucratic forms.

Notwithstanding the challenges, every tool that you can legally employ gives you the upper hand in dealing with your adversaries in litigation. Protecting your assets to the maximum includes the ownership of an International Bank.

Keep in mind that the asset protection planning that I recommend is tax neutral. However, based upon information, reports and case studies that I have witnessed, there are plenty of opportunities to move your asset protection planning up a notch for perfectly legal tax benefits. Here is one example.

Why a Bank?

First, one of the primary reasons of owning an offshore bank, other than generating profits, is that as a foreign entity in an offshore center with strict banking secrecy and financial privacy laws, you are afforded an extra heavy layer of protection. The assets of a bank owned by you will be difficult to discover, due to these strict banking privacy laws. This provides you with a distinct advantage as an owner of an offshore bank against those who wish to make a claim against you and your assets.

Second, unlike individual US investors satisfying burdensome reporting requirements to the IRS, an offshore bank can freely move about assets around the world as it conducts its business. This is a special power and privilege available to the banking industry that simply does not exist to individuals.

If protection of your assets from the sharks is a serious goal, then once your assets have been transferred to a foreign entity, based in a country with strict secrecy laws, future creditors, investigators, and others will have an extremely difficult time locating those assets. This becomes even more the case when you have foreign, nonrelated parties, that actively manage and control the bank on your behalf.

Third, setting up an offshore bank establishes another layer that an aggressive plaintiff must get through in trying to reach your assets. For example, you can establish your offshore bank in one jurisdiction under one name, doing business in another jurisdiction under an assumed named, and have it actively managed by others from yet another jurisdiction. Each layer added to the structure will frustrate someone trying to learn about your assets. This is another technique to gain privacy that is available to you today.

The type of assets you place in an offshore bank include cash, stocks, and business trade secrets. In fact, any type of asset can be placed into the bank. Once you place those assets with the bank, you can truthfully state that you are unaware of the specific assets and how they are being used when a professional management team is managing them.

YOUR TRUST - YOUR BANK

One of the most effective ways of setting up an offshore bank is having an Offshore Trust, from another jurisdiction, own the stock of the offshore bank. That way you do not personally own the stock of the offshore bank. The Trust owns the offshore bank's stock, and the bank is managed as you first established it by your professional team.

There are many top notch management teams following Swiss Banking standards available to manage your bank and meet reporting requirements, all at reasonable costs which will vary depending upon asset amounts and investment activities.

The offshore bank is accountable to you by virtue of your Family Asset Protection Trust as its shareholder, and as the Protector of the Trust you will have the power to control, within limits, the activities of the offshore bank.

Establishing an offshore bank assumes that you have a legitimate reason for the bank in the first place. Simply desiring to protect and preserve your assets is not enough. But if you have a serious desire to conduct your business outside the US, and to actually seek profit opportunities from the banking enterprise, then you can easily meet the legitimate purpose requirement.

Reap the Benefits

Creating and combining onshore activities with offshore activities yields greater asset protection than either one alone. Remember synergy.

You can easily diversify your assets and activities politically and geographically. For example, in some situations you may wish to hold assets in your name, or that of a business corporation in the US for business purposes and to secure loans. A separate Trust may offer some additional asset protection for these individual activities, as we have discussed earlier.

Family Limited Partnerships, or a FLP, can allow you to retain control over other assets. In some cases the partnership can be owned 99% by your Family Asset Protection Trust, and in other situations you can hold assets for gifting purposes to pass to next generations. All along you retain control of the assets.

319

Your offshore bank then invests funds for you, makes investments on behalf of the Trust or Family Limited Partnership, seeks out business, investment, and lending opportunities and even other customers that it brings into the bank. Your Family Asset Protection Trust can be the centerpiece of the structure. Better yet, you can use multiple Family Asset Protections Trusts to hold or control different structures for more diversity.

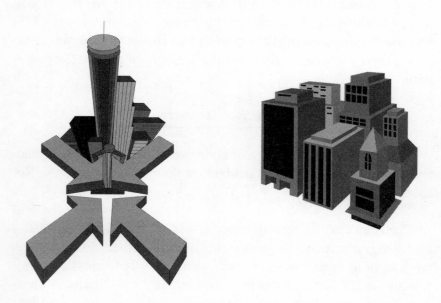

CREATING ROADBLOCKS

All along, by using the concept of synergy, you are creating roadblocks and obstacles which are increasingly difficult to overcome by potentially aggressive litigants. But keep in mind that one of the greatest benefits of the offshore bank is the level of privacy that you will be allowed to gain, due to the banking secrecy laws in the right foreign jurisdiction.

320

Banks vs. IBC's

In the last Chapter, I indicated that an International Business Corporation ("IBC") is a great vehicle for asset protection planning since it has limited foreign reporting requirements and can own property both in and outside of the US. And remember that the reporting and tax requirements inside the US are based upon a controlled foreign corporation and a foreign personal holding company. This is one of the downsides of using an IBC, but balancing all of the factors, it is still an excellent asset protection tool.

Unlike an IBC, if all the requirements are satisfied for an offshore bank, it is afforded certain privileges that an IBC does not have. For example, an offshore bank is excluded from controlled foreign corporation tax penalties. And an offshore bank is exempt from personal holding company taxes pursuant to IRC Sec. 551-555.

Moreover, an offshore bank is exempted from the accumulated earnings tax (Tres.Reg.Sec. 1.532(2)(b)(5)). An offshore bank can defer foreign investment company tax. And, importantly, an international bank duly constituted and properly managed outside the US, will ordinarily be exempt from income outside of the US, since its activities will be conducted internationally through a resident agent or through host-country directors in its charter (Tres.Reg.Sec. 1.8618).

An offshore bank, in the ordinary course of conducting its business affairs outside of the US boundaries, will be exempt from US tax under the asset-used or business-activities test (Tres.Reg.Sec. 1.864-4(c)(5)(ii)).

Finally, offshore banks are afforded special tax treaties advantages. As a general rule, a foreign entity must withhold 30% for income taxes to guarantee tax payment, as a privilege of doing business in the US. However, this requirement can and does change depending on tax treaties between certain jurisdictions and the US.

As you can see, an offshore bank is a special type of corporation afforded certain privileges simply not available to individuals, IBCs, or other entities. But beware, the tax aspects of establishing and owning an offshore bank can be quite complicated.

COST OF BANKING

The cash requirements and cost to establish an offshore bank, excluding legal and tax advice, can vary widely.

Cash requirements for paid-in capital for some jurisdictions can be as low as only $100,000, with annual license fees of only $2,000. The upper end is as great as $5,000,000 of paid-in capital, with $25,000 annual fees. Most jurisdictions fall somewhere in between.

322

Where to Establish Your Bank

Some of the better jurisdictions include Vanuatu and Nauru in the Pacific, and in Grenada and Belize in the Caribbean. These offer the best secrecy laws, combined with low entry fees and minimal annual license fees. They can be managed from those jurisdictions or other jurisdictions, and can generally afford you the opportunity of privacy, asset protection planning, and the prestige of owning a bank.

Belize is one of the few places where private banking is still private. Belize is one of those countries that is bucking the trend of OECD countries attempting to create barriers or even eliminate tax havens to citizens of the US. Belize has created a new set of banking laws designed to keep banking information private and to deter money laundering schemes.

Belize's efforts to stay independent from the pressures of the US appears to be paying off. In 1997, roughly 3,000 offshore companies were registered in Belize, and by the spring of 2000, the numbers had grown to 14,000. The amounts of deposits in the Belize banks have grown dramatically.

Word of Caution

But owning an offshore bank is not without risk factors.

Caution must be used so that you do not infringe on US banking laws by conducting business in the US. You must also use great caution in meeting the regulatory requirements for establishing an offshore bank, particularly as a US citizen. Working with solid, competent tax and legal advisors is critical to avoid

323

the tax-related risks inherent with this aggressive asset protection strategy.

Keep in mind that there are US gift tax issues to consider when transferring assets into a foreign entity, but once you get past these requirements, the growth of the assets in the offshore bank, as long as they're not distributed to you, can continue to grow without income tax obligations.

The potential opportunities are endless, if you are willing to make the commitment and take the plunge into this challenging and rewarding world of International Banking.

YOUR OWN BANK IS ANOTHER GREAT TOOL

The bottom line: if you are looking for another tool in your arsenal of asset protection strategies and wealth preservation, then owning an offshore bank might be for you.

Just think of the opportunities of generating business and profits by the use of your own offshore bank, while all along you are protecting and preserving your wealth. And too, how many of your friends and neighbors have bragging rights that they own their own International Bank?

OFFSHORE BANK ACCOUNTS

Before retiring on the topic of offshore banking, a final word on foreign bank accounts. Offshore bank accounts have their rightful place, but caution is the key.

There certainly are opportunities for practical privacy and

asset protection planning with an offshore account. You have opportunities to place funds outside of the US, making it considerably more difficult for litigation happy claimants trying to reach those funds, particularly if the funds are controlled by your Family Asset Protection Trust as outlined in earlier chapters. Forcing an aggressive litigant to jump through international legal hurdles while trying to make claim against your money in a foreign bank account, generally discourages most plaintiffs and their lawyers.

And too, reaching out to investment opportunities outside of the US is another benefit to an offshore bank account. If you direct your offshore banker to invest in foreign securities with the registration in the bank name and account number, or in the Trust name, opportunities are significantly greater than you will find within the US. This is due, in part, to the increased burden of foreign investment firms having to deal with US citizens and the S.E.C. and IRS burdens attached to this class of investors.

Also, if you are an active investor offshore, then having some of your funds already located in foreign countries can help expedite investment opportunities and minimize US compliance burdens when funds are transferred. Simplicity and privacy is often the motivation.

However, with all of the benefits available to owning an offshore bank account, you should still proceed with caution. Often times, an offshore bank account is opened and maintained with US source income. The funds are opened with a "nod and wink", with the real intentions being tax evasion. This is where a US taxpayer can get into trouble if the accounts are not maintained properly and compliance with IRS regulations are not satisfied.

For example, in a major sweeping tax probe, a Federal Judge recently granted the IRS access to thousands of MasterCard and American Express cardholder's accounts held with offshore banks. Targeted offshore tax havens include the Bahamas, the Cayman Islands, Antigua, and Barbados for the years 1998 and 1999.

The IRS is looking at credit card purchases made by the US cardholders that might reveal they are living beyond their means. While the credit cards are legal, the taxpayers must file forms with the IRS and pay taxes on income earned in the US. The problem is that oftentimes the cardholders fail to report the income or comply with the reporting requirements for a foreign held bank account.

While foreign credit cards attached to offshore bank accounts have legitimate purposes, this investigation, one of the largest in the history targeted by the IRS, will probably result in major tax problems for a huge number of taxpayers.

I am reluctant to give a broad endorsement or guidance to anyone to simply go out and open an offshore bank account for his or her personal use. However, if you satisfy the criteria for maintaining the account, they can be very beneficial for asset protection planning. But if your intentions are to try and evade taxes, then watch out because the civil and criminal ramifications are very real.

Finally, if the steps of establishing and owning multiple and various entities, or international banks, or an offshore bank account don't fit your needs, you might consider the other more drastic options of living overseas, obtaining second passports, or even the final and ultimate step of becoming an expatriate. Are you and your money ready to leave the US?

CHAPTER TWENTY ONE

Living Overseas, Second Passports, & Expatriation

A S YOU KNOW SO WELL, TAXES TAKE A MAJOR bite out of your assets. Not so surprisingly, the top 2% of the major wealth holders pay approximately 30% of all taxes in the US., and the top 15% or so pay around 60% of all taxes. Seems rather unfair, don't you think?

With tax loopholes mostly long gone from the earlier versions of the forever-changing tax code, there is generally little you can do once your assets are income-producing. However, if you are willing to make a significant change in your lifestyle, then there are additional options available to you to help protect and preserve your assets from big tax bites.

BIG BROTHER HAS GOT YOU

The United States is the *only* major industrialized country that taxes its US citizens on their worldwide income. This is true for US citizens even if you live abroad and your income is generated from another country. Regardless of where you live and where you make your money, you are accountable to Uncle Sam as long as you are a US citizen.

If you choose your place of residency wisely, however, you have options to help substantially reduce, or even eliminate, your taxes altogether.

MOVING ABROAD

For some Americans, the American dream is being realized abroad. These adventurous individuals have pooled their money and taken their skills to over 100 different communities around the world. According to the U.S. State Department, more than 3.8 million Americans live aboard every year.

An estimated 250,000 Americans move out of the US each and every year, but most of them are not true tax exiles. The vast majority of the individuals retain their US citizenship. Many of them qualify for tax-free income.

Does any of this stuff have anything to do with the paperwork, taxes and loss of privacy?

Why are so many US citizens leaving their homeland?

As reported in *Money* magazine (July 1994 by Gary Belsky), consider the following: The US is facing a brain drain; 60 percent of Americans state that the US quality of life is degenerating and expatriates seek better lives; expatriates include some of America's wealthiest and most educated native-born citizens; approximately 25% of college educated and 25% of income earners above $50,000 per year have considered leaving the US; more skilled workers are leaving the US than are entering. Increasingly these individuals are searching for the American dream elsewhere.

I will repeat my caveat again that the asset protection planning I recommend is tax neutral. However, based upon information, reports and case studies that I have witnessed, there are opportunities to push your asset protection planning forward for perfectly legal tax benefits. Here are a few more examples based upon those tax experts.

Tax Relief Abroad

In essence, as a non-US resident, you have three options to limit or reduce your taxes. First, you elect to reside in a country that avoids a double taxation by way of a Tax Treaty with that country. Second, you can take up foreign residency on less than a full-time basis. And third, you can elect to expatriate altogether.

Avoiding Dual Taxation

The first option of a "Double Taxation Treaty" is based upon a tax treaty entered into between the US and the country in which

331

US citizens may reside. The tax treaty with that foreign country would supersede, or take precedence, over the US tax code. Basically, the tax treaty would allow you to offset all foreign tax paid against any liability you might have to the IRS while residing in that country.

What this means is that if your foreign taxes are higher than your US taxes, there is no US tax obligation due. If your foreign taxes are lower than the US taxes, you might still owe US taxes unless you can qualify for the "Physical Presence Test", which is covered in the second option below.

While the "Double Tax Treaty" prevents you from being forced to pay taxes twice, it does not help you avoid paying taxes altogether. Obviously this option has certain limitations.

PART TIME TRAVELER

The second option of taking up foreign residency is based upon a physical presence in that country. Can you think of any foreign countries where you might be interested in retiring? Do picture perfect quiet beaches with rolling waves on secluded islands interest you? There are emerging, developing countries with quiet lifestyles that offer tax havens if you can qualify.

This option to reduce or eliminate taxes is based upon Section 911 of the Internal Revenue Code. It requires you to gain foreign residency measured by the number of days you reside in the country, but it does not require you to denounce your US citizenship. If you qualify, you and your spouse can presently earn up to $172,000 in income per year, including a housing allowance of $10,000 each.

There is also a scheduled increase in amounts by 2002 which will allow aggregate amounts of $180,000 to be tax free, including housing allowances. In essence, you and your spouse can set aside these amounts of income free from income taxation if you follow the rules.

Can you and your spouse live comfortably on $180,000 tax free income every year? You bet! In most emerging countries, you can live like a King and Queen with the best housing, maids, cooks, gardeners, and a quality and healthy lifestyle for much, much less.

The first requirement under Code Section 911 is that you must become a resident of a foreign country. There is no requirement that you pay any foreign taxes to that foreign country. Perpetual travelers do not qualify. You must actually take up residency, but of course this does not mean that you cannot travel to other parts of the world from time to time.

The second requirement under the Internal Revenue Code has to do with the source of your income. US pension income, or other US source income will not qualify. However according to good tax sources, it is possible that you can restructure your assets into a foreign corporation to have excludable income. The foreign corporation can then pay a salary to you acting as its asset manager abroad.

This is an ideal structure for a retired person who decides to live abroad and wishes to manage his or her own portfolio. This structure can also work if you are working for other foreign corporations as well.

The third requirement under Code Section 911 has to do with the number of days that you are actually present in the US. The rule appears simple on the face, requiring that you not spend 183 days or more in the US. This rule indicates that you can split your retirement time unequally between your foreign residence and the US. Wintertime in the Caribbean and summers in the US certainly has a tremendous appeal.

But use great caution in interpreting this 183 day rule. In particular, the early years of qualifying for the plan can be tricky if you travel back and forth between your foreign residence and the US. The formula is actually calculated based upon the averages over a three-year period, with certain exceptions. The rule would therefore allow you to return and visit the US for personal, health or other reasons. Therefore, you are not necessarily cutting yourself off from your prior life in the US as long as you meet the test.

A more or less safe number to allow for future needs would be to conservatively limit your stay to only 120 days, even though the rule allows for up to 183. This allows you to stay fewer days one year and more days another year and still be able to qualify for Code Section 911.

There is also a fast track method to qualify in the first year. Under this formula, you can only spend a maximum of 30 days in the US. This is a special exception to the 183-day rule that allows you to qualify right away. After the first year, you can then convert to the more complicated formula set out above.

Keep in mind your goal. If you are willing to change your lifestyle and qualify for foreign tax benefits, there are tremendous tax advantages available to you. Setting aside $180,000 from US taxation and living in a foreign tax-free haven!

What better approach to life is there than obtaining a qualifying residency in the Caribbean, taking vacations to Europe or other parts of the world, and visiting the US for up to a qualifying number of days? All of this is done without losing your US citizenship, allowing you to return at any time, and living the life that you've dreamed of, with tax free income.

If the first two options of the Double Taxation Treaty and the Foreign Residency Test do not meet your objectives to help you protect and preserve your assets, then consider expatriating altogether.

Expatriating

The third option of expatriation is the final step for the US citizen who is so completely fed up with US taxes, litigation, and severe limitations on privacy, that they are willing to leave this country.

The only way that a US citizen can legally eliminate all US income tax and estate taxes, is by completely eliminating all connections to its greedy tax consuming Uncle Sam. In other words, you must completely expatriate yourself altogether from the US.

Expatriation is the ultimate asset protection and wealth preservation plan. However, in recent years, fewer than 800 individuals have expatriated. But those that have done so include businessman John Templeton, of Templeton Funds, when he moved to the Bahamas and saved more than $100,000,000 in taxes in his well-known investment fund.

Other well-known individuals include Campbell Soup heir John "Ippy" Dorrance III moving to Ireland; and Michael Dingman, chairman of Abex and a Ford Motor Company director moving to the Bahamas; Kenneth Dart, heir to the billion-dollar Dart Container fortune moving to the Bahamas; Ted Arison, head of Carnival Cruise Line moving to Israel; and the head of Locktite Corporation, Fred Kreible, moving to the Turks and Caicos. The list goes on and on.

Why do they do it? The reasons are vast and many, but often these individuals are motivated by the unfair burdensome US income and estate tax laws.

Becoming an expatriate means moving abroad so that you are no longer a US resident for federal income tax purposes. This also means that you will need to change your domicile to a suitable foreign country so that you are no longer a US domiciliary for tax purposes. And, you will need to give up your US citizenship so that you are not subject to income taxes on your worldwide income or estate taxes.

Other factors to consider will include making certain that your status is not tainted by the status of your spouse. In other words, your spouse should take the same steps as you do to make sure that your jointly owned property is removed from the jurisdiction of the US. You will then want to make sure that all of your income is derived from foreign sources and that your property is owned in the countries other than the US.

Importantly, I must hammer the point home that you will need to consider the timing of making these property transfers, and consider how it will affect your status as an expatriate. You will need to give consideration as to the beneficiaries of your estate and the tax impact on them if they do not become tax exiles.

So how do you go about giving up your US citizenship?

NEW CITIZENSHIP & PASSPORTS

Unless you are already living abroad, you will need to find a country that is willing to accept you as a resident, in which you and your family will call home. Some countries require a time period to obtain residency, others will require work permits, and in others, you can purchase residency for a set dollar amount or investment into the country.

For example, in Belize, for approximately $45,000, a family of four can instantly obtain residency and a passport for travel. And in Grenada, for approximately $55,000, the same family can instantly obtain permanent citizenship and passport. The Grenada passport is considered a superior passport for travel. (Belize is considered good, but not as good as Granada's).

In Bahamas and in other Caribbean jurisdictions like Nevis and St. Kitts and Dominica, you need only invest monies into the country in the form of a second home or other investment, ranging from $250,000 to $500,000, and you can obtain similar benefits.

The amounts and rules vary from country to country and are in constant flux, and can take weeks to months to complete. What looks good today disappears tomorrow. And all passports are not equal when it comes to traveling to other countries on your new passport. Some countries will allow visa free travel, and others will not. If you wish to return to the US, some passports will be more easily accepted than others. Working with an experienced adviser in this area is critical.

Of course, you can simply go the route of residing in the jurisdiction for a prerequisite time period to qualify without having to pay amounts other than nominal filing fees, if you care to wait.

If you abandon your US citizenship, you are required to make an official denouncement of it, generally through the US Consulates Office by declaring your intentions.

AVOID TAX MOTIVATED APPEARANCES

Keep in mind that good old Uncle Sam may try one last step to get into your pocket before you leave.

Presently, if you have annual income of more than $100,000 per year or assets greater than $500,000, it is assumed that your reasons for expatriating are tax-motivated. If it is determined you are tax-motivated when you expatriate, watch out, because you could end up paying more taxes and penalties.

As a practical matter, to date these retaliatory laws have generally not been applied. Proper advance planning with expert advice can get you around these obstacles.

Once you have denounced your US citizenship, removing yourself from the tax and privacy concerns, you can in many jurisdictions around the world live tax free, in relative privacy without onerous reporting burdens or concerns of litigants trying to remove your money from you. Expatriation can offer you the best of all worlds, and an exotic lifestyle, if you are prepared to make a drastic change in your life.

Dual Citizenship

Many people are automatically entitled to dual citizenship under the laws of various nations.

A growing number of people seek out second citizenship based upon their heritage. For example, Italy and Ireland offer citizenship to American grandchildren of Italian or Irish grandparents. Many other nations have similar programs and sometimes require a residency period.

Your Choice of Paradise

For some individuals, and maybe you are one of them, picking up and leaving the US, whether as a US citizen living abroad earning tax free income from a foreign source, or going the final distance as an expatriate, can offer an exciting challenge to your life. For others looking for more semblance of order in their lifestyle, this may be too drastic of a change. For those happy staying right where they are, plan accordingly.

Whatever you choose do to, you should be aware of your options. Only when you are educated about the alternatives and make a voluntary choice based upon the options, can you be said to be living a free life to its fullest. Maybe that choice is at home, or maybe that choice is abroad. Maybe it is a combination of both.

SEEKING SAFETY

But whatever you do, take the necessary steps, one by one, to protect and preserve your assets.

The goal of wealth preservation is not simply the end result of hoarding money. Instead, it is the preservation and safety of that money that allows you the independence and freedom to make the choices in life that you wish to make. But without the freedom to make those choices, you are nothing more than a prisoner dictated to by someone else.

Next we will look at using life insurance products combined with offshore vehicles to see how you can benefit from another asset protection technique. This is yet another example of aggressive synergy in action.

CHAPTER TWENTY TWO

Offshore Insurance
&
Wealth Preservation

THE OFFSHORE LIFE INSURANCE AND ANNUITY industry is experiencing a surge in positive publicity recently. The increased general attention paid to offshore life and annuity contracts is apparently due, in part, to the attacks made by Congress, the Treasury, and the IRS against offshore Trusts, foreign investment companies, and other offshore structures.

As you see in Appendix A, the reporting requirements can be burdensome for the uninformed. Foreign-issued life insurance and annuity contracts help fill these voids, according to Attorney Michael Heimos of Dean and Heimos in Denver, Colorado.

ESTABLISHED INSURANCE CENTERS

Currently most of this attention centers upon carriers in and products emanating from well-established offshore insurance jurisdictions such as Bermuda, the Isle of Man, and the Cayman Islands.

Soon there may be serious renewed interest in the Bahamas as a viable and important insurance jurisdiction as well. Relatively new insurance legislation applicable to certain companies and products make the Bahamas very attractive.

DOMESTIC VS. OFFSHORE INSURANCE

A major difference between foreign and domestically issued insurance products is the possibility of gaining added asset protection via a foreign product. The common belief that life insurance and annuity products are fully "protected" in the US is very simplistic and, in some instances, quite unfounded.

Of course, most states do confer a preferred status on life and annuity products, exempting these products from creditor claims in varying degrees. But there is no doubt that policy values are generally more protected in offshore jurisdictions.

STATESIDE SHORTCOMINGS

As we discussed in Chapter Nine, each state has a system of debtor protection rules that are designed to shield various amounts of certain assets from the claims of their resident creditors. These protection rules are known as "exemptions" and usually include life insurance and annuity contracts.

You will need to closely examine your state's exemption rules and determine the scope and amount of protection your state provides. Each states varies, but to some extent, your life insurance affords some level of protection from creditors.

First, premiums paid for life insurance products may be subject to state fraudulent conveyance statutes, making premiums paid to insurance carriers subject to creditor's claims. Often such premiums are recoverable by the creditor out of the proceeds of the policy or contract. And, depending upon the state, the burden of proof may only be that a debt or claim existed at the time of the premium payment and is evidence of the intent to defraud.

As crazy as this sounds, the mere fact that a debt existed at the time the premium payment was made, could be sufficient enough to remove your insurance policy from the protection as an item exempted from your creditors.

As for proceeds of death benefits of life insurance policies, a trap for the unwary is that however protective the exemption may seem, its application will often be limited to policies effected for the benefits of certain persons, or regarding the claims of only a certain class of creditors.

In some states, the exemptions that protect the proceeds of life insurance from the creditors of beneficiaries, only apply to those creditors which are owed debts which existed at the time the policy is made available to the beneficiaries. In such situations, the beneficiary's subsequent creditors can obtain redress against policy proceeds; exactly what you may wish to avoid.

And as for annuity contracts, many states allow garnishment of annuity payments, and there is usually only a nominal exemption in respect of each periodic payment. Some states require protection benefits based upon needs, while others offer no protection at all. Some states even expressly exclude annuities from their exemption laws.

Purchasing offshore life insurance products can help avoid many of the shortcomings of asset protection issues, according to Mr. Heimos. Offshore insurance products are often protected by rigid fraudulent disposition legislation. And too, seizure of premiums and proceeds from offshore insurers are generally difficult and burdensome for a creditor, if even possible. The difficulty and expense should be sufficiently intimidating for even the most aggressive creditor to undertake.

Selected Jurisdictions

Topping the list of jurisdictions offering offshore insurance products is Bermuda. The dual application of Bermudan public and private law adds significant asset protection to policy values not matched domestically. These laws add strong asset protection to policies for the benefit of certain family members and address the claims of creditors. On balance, the protection afforded under such provisions are better than those found in many, if not most, US states.

The Isle of Man is located in the Irish Sea, and has a mature insurance industry with a reputation of professionalism and conservatism. The entirety of Manx insurance law is present in public legislation. Manx laws are strong, and impose accountability for attention to asset protection provisions. Violations are punished criminally.

As additional asset protection benefits, the Isle of Man does not enforce US judgments, and any claim initiated in the US must therefore be again retried in the Isle of Man. This is a huge deterrent against litigious creditors.

The Cayman Islands, Channel Islands, and British Virgin Islands all have legislation and protective provisions similar to Bermuda and the Island of Man. While the Cayman Islands and the Channel Islands have a long-established insurance industry with many insurance companies to choose from, the principal shortcoming of the BVIs is that there may be a lack of insurance carriers to choose from.

Barbados has a sophisticated insurance law rivaling any in the world. Its industry is mature and laws are strictly governed by its Insurance Act. There are several layers of protection afforded policyholders and policy assets under the Act. Due to the multiple levels of protection in Barbados, persons interested in asset protection planning should limit their inquires to carriers licensed under the Act and not consider exempt insurers.

In the Bahamas there is recent legislation that specifically applies to offshore insurance business. The Act allows registered carriers to claim an important tax exemption and qualify their products for special asset protection provisions. The Act has specific privacy and accountability provisions. Violations include imprisonment. While the Bahamas are relatively new on the scene with respect to aggressive insurance laws, they appear to have taken great inroads in legislating insurance products for asset preservation since they arrived in this arena.

OFFSHORE BENEFITS

Family wealth preservation, tax-deferred or free investment and tax-efficient wealth transfers, head the list of reasons for purchasing offshore insurance products. Naturally, these products are not for everyone.

Many offshore insurance carriers have self-imposed minimum premium thresholds which only the wealthy can afford. Therefore, oftentimes the best candidates for offshore insurance products are the wealthy businessperson, professional athlete, or professionals who have a high income, plenty of after-tax dollars, and a family to provide for in the event of his or her death.

There are many other practical applications for offshore insurance products. One example is domestic benefit planning (such as split-dollar insurance, welfare benefit plans, etc.) which can be funded through offshore products. Companies and individuals can take advantage of offshore coverage with deductible dollars.

Another interesting use of an offshore insurance product might be as a funding vehicle for a business buy-sell agreement. Due to the asset protection advantages which can be afforded with offshore insurance, this could provide added benefits against business or owner's future creditors.

Offshore Tax Saving Platforms

As outlined for you in Chapter Thirteen, the use of Irrevocable Life Insurance Trusts ("ILIT") is essential to keeping the insurance proceeds out of your estate when you die. Using the same stateside strategies earlier discussed for offshore insurance products, increases your asset protection and wealth preservation.

Another example of using offshore insurance products, and another great example of synergy in action, is outlined below. This example begins with building a "Platform" for using life insurance for income tax planning.

Building a Platform involves the purchase of a life insurance policy, typically from a Swiss life insurance company. The minimum premium is $300,000, providing a death benefit as required under the Tax Code (IRC Section 7702). The policy is then owned either by an ILIT, or by an individual or partnership if you are not concerned about death benefit inclusion in your taxable estate on death.

Another element of the Platform is that the Swiss insurance company, as an investment of the cash value of the policy, acquires some or all of the shares of an International Business Corporation ("IBC"), typically created in the British Virgin Islands.

There are variations of the Platform, but the above is generally the central theme.

Once a Platform has been built, there are numerous tax planning opportunities for the deferral or avoidance of capital gain taxes, income taxes and estate taxes. In addition, on death the life insurance beneficiaries receive a check from the life insurance company, plus the IBC shares, all as part of a tax free life insurance death benefit.

According to the experts in this arena, the above Platform has been successfully used where individuals desired to diversify publicly held stock into shares of other securities and to avoid capital gains.

Other examples for using the Platform include selling businesses by the most tax-advantaged method possible; selling stocks to diversify into more stable investment portfolios; deferring income from dividend paying stock and to transfer wealth to the next generation; deferring gain on the exercise of stock options; and to avoid tax on a non-US business activity.

Working from a properly structured Platform affords many opportunities to avoid taxation.

BEYOND ASSET PROTECTION PLANNING

As you see from some of the above examples, offshore insurance planning has purposes beyond asset protection planning. Combining those business purposes with asset protection strategy can provide a strong wealth preservation strategy. Adding the above techniques as a supplement, not necessarily as a stand-alone plan, is truly a major tool in your asset protection planning arsenal.

As a final word on using stateside and offshore asset protection planning, we would not complete our mission if confidentiality issues were not addressed. Included with the tools outlined in this guide are important and essential ingredients. Follow these steps with confidence and purpose, and do it confidently without advertising your plan.

The last chapter leaves you with a final word on confidentiality.

CHAPTER TWENTY THREE
The Final Word:
Confidentiality

WITH BIG BROTHER LOOKING OVER YOUR SHOULder daily, living in the information age with data and reports available on your living and spending habits, why would you want to expose yourself more and tell your potential adversaries how you have designed your wealth preservation plan?

Remember that a friend today can turn out to be your worst enemy tomorrow. Bad things can and do happen to good people, and things change in the scope of relationships. The only constant in life is change: learn to adapt to it.

SILENCE

Once you have established a Plan B, keep it to yourself. Do not share it with your friends at the next cocktail party.

Forget about bragging rights, notwithstanding my earlier suggestions to the contrary. Keep your papers and financial information beyond the reach of someone looking to be nosy into your affairs. Do not save it on your computer. Do not make it easy for someone to take apart and poke holes into what you have worked hard to accomplish.

RECOVERABLE INFORMATION

I recall the case for Mr. G. He was certain that his business partner was stealing from him. All business records were recorded on a computer, but when the partner and Mr. G went their separate ways, the business partner deleted all computer data and destroyed all hard paper copy evidence, to cover his tracks.

Notwithstanding the stealth efforts of the crooked partner, we were able to send the now "empty" computer to a special data recovery service in California, which could locate "shadows" of erased data on computer hard drives that allowed data to be restored. When we presented the supposedly erased records to the business partner at his deposition, both his lawyer and he went crazy believing the records no longer existed.

Needless to say, the case quickly settled favorably for Mr. G.

Privileged Communications and Confidentiality

Working through a qualified legal adviser is essential. Only through an attorney can you have the strictest, privileged communications and confidentiality in your activities.

If you walked into my office tomorrow and retained me to assist you in establishing a "Plan B" for asset protection, it would be in strictest confidence. With rare exception, for example, discussing specific plans to commit a serious crime, an attorney is prohibited from disclosing conversations. He must keep shared information behind closed doors. I could lose my license as an attorney and become subject to civil, and perhaps criminal, sanctions for disclosing our meeting discussions.

While there are other areas of privileged communications, for example with certified public accountants, that privilege is much more limiting and weaker than the attorney-client privilege. The better procedure is for me to retain the accountant as a consultant on your behalf. This allows the privilege to become stronger since a lawyer retained the accountant.

Telephone Calls

Telephone calls can lay your life bare before people you least wish to know your business. Always assume someone is listening to every word you say on the telephone. Never discuss anything on the telephone that you would not want a government agent or police officer to hear.

TAPE RECORDINGS

Be cautious of someone with a tape recording device on their person.

I recently had a client in the privacy of my office that was confronted with serious personal and business problems. He was desperate. Unbeknownst to me, during our conference he had a recording device hidden on his person to record our conversations *"just in case"*. In case of what, I do not know. I only learned of this hidden device after our meeting was finished and, needless to say, I was very surprised. Obviously I had nothing to hide, but the episode just highlights the fact that these things can and do happen when you least expect it.

FAXES

And be careful when faxing information. Telephone fax numbers can and do get changed or mixed up. And even when numbers remain the same, you can never be certain about the peering eyes that might exist on the other end.

LONG DISTANCE TELEPHONE CALLS

Telephone calls, especially long distance calls, are all recorded and easily obtained. Your local telephone and cell phone providers often keep records of these calls for years as well. If you do not want your telephone calls known to others, use a public telephone. Or, if you prefer, use anonymous cellular and long distance telephone providers which are available for a fee.

Mail

The monitoring and opening of mail by police, intelligence agencies and the Postal Service is legal and condoned under numerous circumstances, even without a search warrant. This is particularly true when mail is received from tax haven countries which the government considers a "source area". Using mail drops outside of the US and picking up this mail when you visit this country, is a reliable and affordable option.

Computer Security

Computer security is an oxymoron as far as I am concerned. Even with some of the encryption software available today, privacy is highly suspect. If the software available today was so sophisticated to guarantee privacy, then how would hackers routinely gain entry into sensitive government and big business computer systems and create so much havoc on personal computer systems connecting to major Internet providers?

If you do not want your private information known over the Internet, watch what you say and to whom you send it.

Recently, I read in the Denver Post of a computer hacker that breached Western Union's computer system and downloaded credit card data for 15,700 customers. What makes this security breach particularly bothersome is that Western Union is owned by First Data Corp. of Atlanta, which is supposed to be one of the preeminent computer experts for safekeeping financial records. So, how safe and private do you *really* believe that your financial information is when you sleep tonight?

SOCIAL SECURITY NUMBERS

Finally, and perhaps most importantly, few people have a legitimate need for your social security number. With your social security number becoming the ultimate link to each and everything you own, why give it out to sources that really do not need it. It amazes me the irrelevant number of times it is requested. Simply say no to giving it out, unless it becomes absolutely necessary, and then think twice.

PRIVACY

Remember, it is not just criminals that have a need for privacy. I believe that the majority of people are honest, like you and me, and simply desire to maintain the privacy of what is left of our personal business.

Why are Americans so willing to give up our constitutionally protected right of privacy, and allow any prying eye snoop into what is none of their damn business? Why does someone assume that because you seek to live a private life, you must being doing something wrong or illegal? Is nothing that you think or believe sacred anymore? Does your life need to become a soap opera for the entertainment of some deprived, ignorant jerk? Do you need to assist an adversary with proving what he believes is his litigation right against you?

Where does it all end if you do not take action to reduce this big brother mentality?

FINAL NOTES

I HAVE SPENT APPROXIMATELY TWO DECADES OF working with individuals, probably very similar to you, who have made or lost large sums of money during their life. No doubt, the happier ones are those that have retained their hard earned money.

The smartest clients that I have had the opportunity to work with are those who started at the simplest and basic level of asset protection planning and grew their structure as their asset base grew or their circumstances changed. I am also pleased to say that I have learned much from them as well.

Now You Have It

The first part of this guide was founded upon the basics of stateside asset protection planning and wealth preservation. I provided you with an introduction and overview of commonly used tools for everyday life, whether it is in your personal or business relationships. You were probably familiar with some of these tools, but you were introduced to new techniques and how to best apply them.

The second part of this book was based upon protecting and preserving your assets from natural disasters. This segment provided you with an overview of how to plan for disabilities and the inevitable, death. This is an important part of protecting and preserving your assets if you are serious about dealing with some of the inevitable natural disasters that life can bring you and your loved ones.

Importantly, I tried to encourage you to think of ways to combine these stateside tools with offshore planning. A successful asset protection plan integrates stateside estate planning techniques with offshore asset protection strategies.

The third and final segment of this book, is undoubtedly what I believe to be the most exciting part of asset protection planning and wealth preservation. It simply and importantly addressed many different aspects of advanced asset protection planning for the serious-minded individual. The first two segments of the book laid an introduction for the third section, but it clearly stands on its own. Using offshore tools for asset protection planning is by far the best way to protect and preserve assets.

Integrating stateside strategies with offshore techniques affords you the very best protection available worldwide today.

SYNERGY

The use of tools and techniques together is an important part of the third and final segment.

Importantly, you witnessed how some of the most aggressive individuals preserve their wealth and how you can use these same tools today as well. This advanced and aggressive level of asset protection planning is perfectly legal. Being without these techniques leaves you naively vulnerable in a world where wealth accumulation is often lost much quicker than it is created.

PLAN OFFENSIVELY

Why a case for aggressive asset protection planning? Litigation has run amuck in the US. The greater your asset level, the fact that you own, run, or operate a business, or by virtue of being a professional, all increase your likelihood of being sued. And all litigation is not well grounded in good facts or law; and a judge or jury gone amuck can devastate your lifestyle. One lawsuit could literally wipe you out.

INTEGRATED PLANNING

Remember, a good asset protection plan only starts with stateside planning. Do not forget that an aggressive asset protection plan goes beyond stateside planning and uses Trust planning techniques that are more advantageous than those found in our own legal system.

Use a Family Asset Protection Trust as the next level of wealth preservation if you are truly serious about protecting and preserving your assets. This does not mean sending your money off to distant places and losing control of your money. Instead it means using the synergy of various legal entities and retitling the assets and managing and controlling them wisely.

The structure of a Family Asset Protection Trust integrates estate planning and is based upon sound and legitimate business and personal objectives. The basic structure of holding assets in a Family Limited Partnership that you control as General Partner can be quickly expanded upon using multiple partnership and corporate entities for wealth preservation and even tax planning reasons. By having your Family Asset Protection Trust structure properly in place, you are then positioned to act quickly in the event of a catastrophe and not worry about fraudulent conveyance laws that can unwind your plan.

ONE SIZE DOES NOT FIT ALL

There are correct ways (and incorrect ways) to establish and use these aggressive tools, so retaining competent legal advice is critical to the health and well being of your plan. Jurisdictions around the world vary widely, and so do individual's goals. A one-size-fits-all plan should generally be disregarded.

THINK INTERNATIONAL

An offshore bank has distinct advantages in the arsenal of asset protection planning. While the steps are not simple, they do have their place if you are serious about privacy and asset protection planning.

Living overseas can and does have its advantages if you are prepared to greatly change your lifestyle. Being a resident of another country receiving income from a foreign source allows you to receive a healthy income tax free, and still not cut your strings entirely from your friends and family at home. However, if you are really ready to go the full distance, then becoming an expatriate and leaving the good old US offers the last and final step in avoiding litigation American style and becoming a free soul gaining levels of privacy that you can only dream of.

The use of offshore insurance products has its place for the right individuals. Not only can there be tax advantages to these tools, but the asset protection opportunities can far exceed what can be found in most US jurisdictions. Opportunities exist world-wide for life insurance and annuity products that you cannot find at home.

CONFIDENTIALITY

And finally, keeping your asset plan confidential is essential.

How else can I say it, but keep your mouth shut! Do not advertise the steps that you have taken to secure your most private matters. Do not give away what you seek to preserve. Your best friend today can become your worst enemy tomorrow. Why provide him or her tools to destroy everything you have accomplished? Keep your asset protection plan to yourself.

This book is designed for the layperson and not so much for the technically minded. Nonetheless, professionals acting in the discipline of law, accounting and asset management will find it a useful aid in providing solid advice to their clients. Use it well, with legal intentions.

ACT NOW!

Importantly, an accumulation of wealth provides you with not only personal freedom to choose, but also to do great things during the short time you are in this world. A motto placed over 600 years ago in one of the magnificent paintings in the Pitti Palace in Florence, Italy reads: *"All fortune is illusory, it passes and does not last. Merit and virtue last and do not pass away."* Might you too do great things as part of your legacy.

Too often, most people fail to give any serious thought to protecting what they have worked long and hard for until they are confronted with a problem. Then, unfortunately, there is little they can do because they have waited too long. I hope you take the time to not only give serious thought about how to protect those assets you have been working so diligently to provide you and your family for, but most importantly, do it now.

If you gain nothing else from this book, let it be that the key to asset protection planning and wealth preservation is that you must act **<u>now</u>**, before it is too late, if you are serious in protecting and preserving your money and property. And remember the power of synergy.

Synergy now. Synergy now. I've got it!

What are your goals? Is it important to you or your family to achieve these goals? Are you ready to act **<u>now</u>**? Then do it! Get up from this book and begin today executing your plan.

HOW TO CONTACT US

WHILE I HAVE TRIED TO AVOID SHAMELESS self-promotion in this book, please allow me just a little wiggle room. If your personal goals are above-board, legal, and you do not ask that I perform unethical maneuvers to assist you with your own asset protection and wealth

Here is the shameless self-promotion part.

preservation planning, I would look forward to discussing your goals and objectives. Naturally, this will be in the strictest degree of privacy.

I have taken great effort to locate and find some of the best minds to help you accomplish your wealth preservation goals. These contacts and resources should all be part of the package since I believe that you cannot be everything to everybody. Building a quality aggressive team, working together, is the hallmark of establishing a good asset protection plan.

You can contact me as follows:

David A Tanzer
David A. Tanzer & Associates, P.C.
2121 N. Frontage Rd. W., # 209
Vail, CO 81657
Tel. 970-476-6100
Fax. 970-476-6109
Website: DavidTanzer.com

APPENDIX "A"

REPORTING REQUIREMENTS FORMS LIST

FOREIGN ASSET PROTECTION TRUSTS:

DOMESTIC GRANTOR TRUSTS FOR US TAX PURPOSES

Form 1041	US Income Tax Return for Estates and Trusts
Form 709	US Gift Tax Return

FOREIGN GRANTOR TRUSTS FOR US TAX PURPOSES

Form 1040NR	US Nonresident Lien Income Tax Return
Form 1040	(Schedule B, III Q8) Interest & Ordinary Dividend
Form 3520	Annual Return to Report Transactions with Foreign Trusts & Receipts of Certain Foreign Gifts
Form 3520A	Annual Information Return of Foreign Trust with a US Owner
Advisory Form	Appointment of US Agent
Form 709	US Gift Tax Return

PARTNERSHIPS:

DOMESTIC PARTNERSHIPS

Form 1065	US Partnership Return of Income

369

Form 709   US Gift Tax Return

FOREIGN PARTNERSHIPS

Form 8865   Information Return of US Persons Respect
to Certain Foreign Partnerships
Form 1065   US Partnership Return of Income
Form 709   US Gift Tax Return

CORPORATIONS:

DOMESTIC CORPORATIONS

Form 1120   US Corporation Income Tax Return

FOREIGN CORPORATIONS

Form 926   Return of US Transferor of Property to a
Foreign Corporation
Form 1120-F   US Income Tax Return for Foreign Cor-
poration
Form 5471   Information Return of US Person with
Respect to Certain Foreign Corporations
Form 5472   Information Return of a 25% Foreign-
Owned US Corporation or a Foreign Cor-
poration Engaged in a US Trade or Busi-
ness

Foreign Bank or Investment Accounts:

TD F 90-22.1	Report of Foreign Bank & Financial Accounts
Form 1040 (Schedule B, III, Q 7)	Interest & Ordinary Dividends

Miscellaneous:

Form 56	Notice Concerning Fiduciary Relationship
FSA-153	US Department of Agricultural Foreign Investment Disclosure Act Report
Form 8288	US Withholding Tax Return for Dispositions by Foreign Persons of US Real Property Interests
Form 8804	Annual Return for Partnership Withholding Tax
Form 8805	Foreign Partner's Information Statement of Section 1446 Withholding Tax
Form 8813	Partnership Withholding Tax Payment (Section 1446)
Form 1042	Annual Withholding Tax Return for US Source Income of Foreign Persons
Form 8300	Report of Cash Payments Over $10,000 Received in a Trade or Business
Form 4789	Currency Transaction Report
Form 4790	Report of International Transport of Currency or Monetary Instruments

Index

375

Q

Q-Tips 14, 193
qualified terminal interest trust 193
qualified transfer 228
Quantum Merit 85

R

recourse 74, 140, 164
recoverable information 20, 354
removing 191, 256, 309, 339
replacement residence 122, 123
report 36, 207, 284, 285, 326, 369, 371
reporting 36, 140, 156, 285, 290, 312, 316, 317, 321, 326, 339, 343, 369
reporting requirements
     36, 156, 285, 290, 312, 313, 316, 317, 318, 321, 326, 343, 369
representative 184, 186, 211
reside 101, 137, 144, 179, 331, 332
residence 58, 122, 123, 141, 157, 158, 263, 306, 334
residency 288, 330, 331, 332, 333, 335, 337, 339
resident 321, 331, 333, 336, 337, 344, 363
resolutions 8, 63, 65
restrain 243
retirement 23, 92, 93, 119, 131, 145, 182, 192, 199, 223, 239, 242, 334
risk
     34, 49, 63, 64, 68, 163, 164, 168, 211, 239, 262, 303, 304, 305, 309, 323
role 66, 68, 140, 180
rule 34, 80, 91, 93, 132, 200, 202, 260, 322, 334

S

S-Corp 11, 120, 121, 127, 157, 262, 263, 303, 304, 305
S.E.C. 325
safety 20, 48, 233, 340
safety nets 48
sailing 45, 46
saving 183, 308
second homes 158, 190
secrecy 236, 90, 293, 317, 320, 323
Section 911 332, 333, 334
security 20, 24, 32, 54, 93, 110, 130, 145, 167, 211, 357, 358
segregating 18, 299